What people are saying about

Libertarian Paganism

Finally, an author that is tackling this subject I've seen in Asatru/ pagan circles for the last 23 years of my spiritual journey. Logan explores the liberty connection to not only Asatru, but within any pagan traditions across the spectrum.
Devin Rogers, founder and Gothi of New Vinland Temple

This book offers a general introduction to paganism and libertarianism for those who are not already familiar with both or either, but it also describes the author's unique journey and the ethical and philosophical underpinnings of this viewpoint. This is very timely, given the levels of intolerance, stereotyping, political and social conflict, misunderstandings, and rising authoritarianism that plagues both paganism and wider society. This book offers an alternative perspective that recognizes the sovereign rights of the individual to determine their own path and live a spirituality freely, but without negatively impacting those same rights for anyone else.
Luke Eastwood, author of *The Journey and The Druid's Primer*

T0007677

Libertarian Paganism

Freedom and Responsibility in
Nature-Based Spirituality

Libertarian Paganism

Freedom and Responsibility in Nature-Based Spirituality

Logan Albright

**MOON
BOOKS**

Winchester, UK
Washington, USA

JOHN HUNT PUBLISHING

First published by Moon Books, 2023
Moon Books is an imprint of John Hunt Publishing Ltd., No. 3 East Street, Alresford
Hampshire SO24 9EE, UK
office@jhpbooks.net
www.johnhuntpublishing.com
www.moon-books.net

For distributor details and how to order please visit the 'Ordering' section on our website.

Text copyright: Logan Albright 2022

ISBN: 978 1 80341 360 0
978 1 80341 361 7 (ebook)
Library of Congress Control Number: 2022943552

A CIP catalogue record for this book is available from the British Library.

Design: Lapiz Digital Services

UK: Printed and bound by CPI Group (UK) Ltd, Croydon, CR0 4YY
Printed in North America by CPI GPS partners

We operate a distinctive and ethical publishing philosophy in
all areas of our business, from our global network of authors to
production and worldwide distribution.

Contents

This book is dedicated to my mother, Judy, a constant source of inspiration and the wisest woman I've ever known.

Also by Logan Albright

Conform or Be Cast Out:
The (Literal) Demonization of Nonconformists
ISBN 9781789048421

Our Servants, Our Masters:
How Control Masquerades as Assistance
ISBN 9781630691882

Acknowledgements

I wish to thank Trevor Greenfield and the entire publishing team at Moon Books for their continued faith in me as a writer and for their tireless efforts to help promote my previous book. To Matt and Terry Kibbe, I owe a tremendous amount of gratitude, not only for providing me with gainful employment over the last decade, but for tolerating and encouraging my quixotic dream of writing books for a living, and for providing me with every opportunity to market both myself and the products of my pen. Thanks to New Vinland's Devin Rogers for some very productive dialogue about libertarian paganism, as well as for reviewing the manuscript, and to the Firefly House for putting up with me as their token libertarian. Finally, my deepest appreciation for my parents, Gary and Judy Albright, without whom nothing that I have accomplished would have been remotely possible.

Introduction

My Personal Journey Through Libertarian Paganism

Hello, my name is Logan, and I'm a pagan libertarian. Or maybe I'm a libertarian pagan, or maybe it doesn't matter. For a long time, I thought these two things were independent facets of my personality, separate beliefs with no real relation to one another. As I continued my studies, however, I began to realize that maybe the fact that I was interested in two fairly obscure, non-mainstream belief systems was not a coincidence. Pagans tend not to give much credence to coincidence anyway, preferring to regard simultaneous happenings as synchronistic signs from the universe rather than the result of pure random chance. Over time, I have met other libertarian pagans, their presence strengthening my view that there is more going on here than meets the eye. Nor do I think it's just a personal proclivity for fringe ideologies. There are plenty of wacky belief systems that I reject totally as nonsensical or backwards. Being a minority opinion is not enough to attract my attention. There is something fundamental to the nature of these two systems of belief that led me to seek them out independently.

The thesis of this book is that libertarians and pagans are natural allies. If I'm being honest, my intended audience probably resembles pagans vaguely interested in libertarianism more than it does libertarians vaguely interested in paganism, but I will obviously welcome any reader who happens to pick up the book. I hope you will find something here that will be useful, or at least thought provoking in the development of that personal philosophy which we all need to continually work on if we are to live lives of meaning and purpose.

I was a libertarian before I was a pagan. While I was in college, I discovered that, not only did I possess a reasonably coherent political philosophy without realizing it, but that it was an unusual one not shared by most other people. I latched onto libertarianism with both hands, read every book I could find, and became increasingly convinced that the conventional wisdom surrounding politics was getting an awful lot wrong. These ideas ultimately inspired me to study economics in graduate school, move to Washington, DC, and pursue a career trying to advance the cause of individual freedom and personal liberty. While detractors of libertarianism frequently accuse it of being an adolescent ideology that one soon grows out of, my subsequent years of experience have only solidified my commitment to the idea that a society that disregards the freedom of its citizens is not one worth living in. Maybe I'm just a case of arrested development, but if so, I'm happy enough to stay that way.

Paganism came to me later. I have always been skeptical of, yet not without a certain fascination for religion and spirituality. As a boy, I tended towards extreme left-brain rationalism and an adherence to the rules of formal logic, as well as a commitment to the objective nature of the universe. My parents were generally agnostic, so I was allowed to pursue my own adventures in belief without interference or pressure to conform to one particular tradition or faith. I read the Bible and scoffed at its logical fallacies and contradictions. I attended church a few times and found that it left me feeling empty and bored. I read up on a handful of other religions, but their beliefs and dogmas always struck me as arbitrary and without basis in reality as I experienced it.

On the other hand, I had always been fascinated by fantasy and the idea of magic, especially the darker side of those themes. Secret societies, dusty books of arcane lore, witches, ghosts, and things that go bump in the night always held a special place in my otherwise logical mind, and there was a part of me that refused to believe in a world without a hidden (or "occult") side waiting to be discovered.

Of course, after the shattering of a number of cherished childhood illusions, I contented myself with dismissing all those innermost thoughts as purely wishful thinking until I stumbled upon a source of inspiration in an unlikely place, one that set me off on a journey into paganism that would take over a decade to fully blossom.

In October of 2007, I was browsing in a Boston branch of the now-extinct Borders Books, perusing a table carefully curated for Halloween. It will come as no surprise to the reader that Halloween is my favorite holiday. I was looking for some scary stories or something else appropriately spooky to add to the already magical New England atmosphere at that time of year, and I was drawn to a book with an almost entirely dark cover save for two menacing yellow eyes and the word *Monsters*. I picked it up, expecting some cheesy catalogue of mythical beings, and was surprised to find an elaborate and serious treatment of supposedly fictional entities ranging from vampires and werewolves to fairies and demons. The author was a man called John Michael Greer, identified on the back cover as the head of the American Order of Bards, Ovates, and Druids. I didn't really know that druids were real, but he certainly looked the part, with his chest-length beard. Most interesting of all, the final pages of the book were filled with practical instructions for magic spells designed to banish hostile spirits. What!? Magic spells? Despite much wishing and hoping, I had always thought magic was a purely literary invention, but here was a real-life druid teaching me supposedly real magic with utter seriousness. My mind was blown, and my lifelong obsession with occultism had begun.

I spent about a decade reading and exploring first the ideas of western occultism and ceremonial magic, then the spiritual backbone that underlies many practitioners of this curious art, mostly focusing on Wicca and Druidry. I studied in solitary fascination, aware that my interests were arcane and somewhat taboo. For the most part, I kept my mouth shut and my gradually developing views to myself. Eventually, it occurred to me to see whether anyone else out there felt the same way I did, and I was delighted and amazed to discover a whole community lurking just beneath the surface of "ordinary" society. The people I encountered were so kind, welcoming, and generous with their knowledge, that I soon began to embrace my newfound pagan identity openly. I also found that there was a lot of philosophical overlap between these interesting folks who shunned society's demands for conformity while vehemently rejecting authoritarianism with the libertarian community to which I already belonged. We may vote differently and have policy disagreements, but underneath any surface level squabbles lies a deep respect for personal freedom and self-expression. And yet these two communities, so similar in many ways, tended to regard one another with the skepticism or hostility born of media-created stereotypes. That is, if they regarded each other at all, which they generally didn't. My hope is to dispel some of the ignorance and prejudice that has plagued both libertarians and pagans over the years, while demonstrating that they would be better suited as allies than as enemies.

The timing for such a book has, I think, never been better. Americans are currently floundering through a transitional period of deep anxiety and uncertainty. Support for the major monotheistic religions is in decline, and yet the rational enlightenment promised by the new atheist movement seems to have left many feeling hollow and unfulfilled. A purely materialistic viewpoint, it turns out, is not making people happy, as they struggle to find purpose and meaning in their lives. In their quest for belonging, some misguided people have turned to conspiracy theories or violent mobs. The optimist in me believes that this is a temporary condition, however, and that sooner or later people will find a more productive outlet for the very human need for community, as indeed many already are. For the last several decades, the number of Americans who identify as Wiccans, druids, heathens, or other pagans has been steeply rising. As of 2018, survey data from the Pew Research Center and others put the number at roughly 1.5 million[1], which would make paganism more popular than Presbyterianism. Granted, paganism comprises a wide variety of different traditions, whereas Presbyterianism is one denomination of the still very dominant religion of Christianity, but given that the same surveys only found 8,000 pagans in the U.S. in 1990, the increase is a remarkable one.

The oppressive false-duality of monotheism versus atheism that so many young people are rejecting is mirrored in the polarized and polarizing left-right divide on the political spectrum. It's a hard thing to be told you have to pick a side, and that by doing so you will inevitably draw the hatred and revulsion of many of your friends and colleagues, regardless of which you choose. Fortunately, you don't have to do any such thing. Just as paganism represents a third option with respect to religion, libertarianism is a political philosophy that is fundamentally neither conservative nor progressive. While some libertarians are more sympathetic to the right and others to the left, on the whole they reject the entire concept of the spectrum. Libertarians argue that the real divide is not between conservatives and progressives, but between authoritarians and anti-authoritarians. From the perspective of the individual, a left-wing authoritarian is not much different from a right-wing authoritarian if they are not allowing you to live your life and make your own choices.

It seems to me that the moment is ripe for exploring these two "third ways" between traditional power structures. The hunger for it is there, and I hope to do my own small part in helping it along by pointing out that, no, you don't have to believe what they want you to believe, where they can represent the church, the government, your neighbors, the social media mob, or corporate America with equal appropriateness. You are an individual, and your life is yours to live, not anybody else's. It's incumbent upon you to decide what that life is going to look like and how to manifest your beliefs in the world.

I imagine that critics of this book will accuse me of attempting to coopt a spiritual movement and bend it to fit a particular set of political ends. This would be an immensely cynical and dishonest thing to do, and I can certainly understand why such an approach might provoke some extreme reactions. Let me assure the reader, then, that this is not my goal. Paganism is not a proselytizing religion, and trying to "convert" people runs counter to a fair few libertarian principles. Neither am I trying to tell pagans what to believe with respect to political philosophy. I am all too aware that libertarians are not always popular in pagan circles, and that's okay. Everyone is free to find their own answers to the big questions of life and how to live together in society. If you think the answers libertarianism give to those questions are bad ones, that's okay too. I'm not looking for recruits, I promise. Instead, this book is simply my way of working out some similarities I've noticed in the two worldviews in the hope that some readers – people like myself if I can dare hope that such people exist – may find it useful in discovering their own path. You don't have to be a libertarian to be a pagan, nor do you have to be a pagan to be a libertarian. But if you have individualist tendencies and you're looking for answers, it is my hope that you will find something here that will help you in your search.

An Ye Harm None, Do What Ye Will
The Wiccan Rede

A Note on Terminology

Throughout this book, I'll be spelling the word "libertarian" with a lowercase L, in order to distinguish the philosophy of libertarianism from the activities and membership of the Libertarian Party, an American political party founded in 1971. While the Libertarian Party professes to represent the beliefs of libertarians, and while many libertarians do belong to the Party, the two terms are not synonymous. The nature of politics means that a Party must have an official platform, which will necessarily exclude a great number of people who would otherwise regard themselves as inclined towards libertarianism, and it is my intention to address a broader audience, many of whom would not appreciate being conflated with any political advocacy group, and neither do I want this work to come across as an endorsement of any such group. Furthermore, I have no business nor desire to tell people how they should vote or which legislation they should support. This is a book about ideas related to spirituality, ethics, and one's general worldview. How or if one chooses to put that worldview into practice, through political means or otherwise, is one's own concern.

In the spirit of even-handedness, I've also chosen to spell "pagan" and "paganism" with lower case Ps. This serves the rather useful purpose of avoiding any implication that paganism (at least the kind of paganism I'm interested in) is any sort of organized or monolithic religion equivalent to the traditionally capitalized Catholicism, for example. There is no Pope of paganism, nor is there a pagan equivalent to the Bible. Instead, what I'm talking about is a loose set of beliefs and practices, which I will be more specific in defining a bit later on. I'll also be using a lower-case G when talking about god or gods. Paganism is generally polytheistic, so to use the capital letter as Christians do to denote a single supreme being would be inappropriate here, but its omission should not be interpreted as a lack of respect for the divine in all its manifestations.

I also want to note that my use of the word "paganism" generally refers to a set of traditions found in Western Europe, most popularly manifesting in Wicca and its offshoots, with some nods to the Druidry of the British Isles and the Heathenism of the Nordic countries. This is not to imply that other varieties of paganism do not exist in many different cultures around the world, or to disrespect any of those belief systems. There are certainly plenty of practitioners of what we might call paganism among the indigenous peoples of North and South America, Asia, Australia, Africa, and the islands in the Caribbean. The reason why I don't talk much about these is primarily my own ignorance. My reading and personal practice, though extensive in a narrow sort of way, has not yet sufficiently encompassed these native traditions to which I do not ethnically or spiritually belong, and if I were to try to speak on them at any length for the sake of inclusion, I would invariably get things embarrassingly wrong. I hope the reader will therefore understand the scope of the discussion that follows, and trust that I mean no malice or marginalization by limiting my comments to traditions with which I am actually familiar.

Finally, in the pages that follow I'm going to try to avoid the use of the word "politics" as much as possible. The term politics generally refers to the practice of campaigning for public office, crafting and voting on legislation, lobbying government officials, and engaging in public propaganda in support or opposition to any of the above. Personally, I view the political sphere as one which is inherently corrupt and corrupting of those who partake too deeply of its poisonous temptations, and it would displease me greatly to taint my spiritual beliefs by linking them to the base world of the self-serving, palm-greasing, back-room-dealing political insider.

I prefer to think of libertarianism, rather than as a set of political positions, as a philosophy. However, recognizing that the term "philosophy" is rather too broad to be useful, and also that libertarianism is, for better or worse, inextricably concerned with various matters of a political nature, I will compromise by using the phrase "political philosophy", with the understanding that one's philosophy can inform one's politics, but not the other way around. Vote for whomever you like, if you vote at all; just leave me out of it.

Chapter 1

An Introduction to Libertarian Paganism

At first glance, political philosophy and spirituality or religion may seem like strange bedfellows. After all, the first is concerned with mundane earthly matters like fiscal and monetary policy, while the other is concerned with deep truths about the universe and the human condition itself. Just as the old truism says that science and religion should not attempt to invade each other's respective domains, so it could also be said that politics has no place in spirituality, and vice versa. But in actual fact, the distinction between religion and philosophy is a largely artificial one.

I have always been rather puzzled by the idea that religious views should be held sacred while political views should not. There is a cultural taboo against mocking people's religious beliefs and we are told that we have to respect everyone's different conception of what god is like and how best to worship him (or her, or them). Yet no such taboo exists for beliefs about very important things like war, criminal justice, immigration, health care, and education. Why not? I suppose there is some sense that a person's religion is more deeply held and personal than a person's view on the role of government in society. Religion is regarded as an intrinsic part of who a person is, an immutable characteristic like race or sexual orientation. By contrast, there seems to be a sense that a person's political views are somehow voluntarily chosen, as if we could swap out various philosophies of good and evil, right and wrong, like we change our clothes, so long as these ideas do not involve any gods. I suspect it also has something to do with the history of religious persecution around the globe, something certainly to be taken seriously and something which we should absolutely try to avoid if at all possible.

Yet, I've never subscribed to this dualistic view. My own convictions about the value of human freedom seem to me as personal and integral to my being as any religion could be, nor could I change them even if I wanted to. To assert that my unshakable belief in the intrinsic value of human freedom is less sacred than someone else's belief about which foods they can eat or how many times a day they are required to pray is, at the very least, insulting. And there's certainly no shortage of people who have been tortured and killed for their political views. A personal philosophy, whether concerned with divinity or not, is surely something both special and important. From that perspective, it seems entirely appropriate to talk about two quite distinct philosophies and examine how they relate to and complement each other. This is not to say, however, that I object to my beliefs, religious or otherwise, being mocked. One thing pagans and libertarians have in common is that we tend to have a pretty good sense of humor, both about the world and about ourselves. If you want to mock me, go right ahead. Just do me a favor and make it funny.

What Is Paganism?

Paganism is difficult to define, because it does not comprise a single belief system, but rather is a blanket term for a whole family of traditions and practices from around the world. Originating as a Roman slur for the old-fashioned beliefs of rural non-Christians, the Latin word *paganus* simply means "country dweller," and was used to refer to those who continued to worship Jupiter, Venus, Mars, and Helios over the more fashionable Yahweh and Jesus Christ. Over time, the word "pagan" became a more general term for practitioners of ancient, polytheistic religions largely suppressed by the increasing dominance of Christianity around the globe. The

Greek and Roman gods were considered pagan, but so were the Norse, Celtic, and Egyptian pantheons, as well as a variety of folk practices from around the world not necessarily associated with any well-defined tradition.

Over the years, the meaning of paganism has both expanded to incorporate a wider variety of traditions, while simultaneously contracting towards a shared set of implicit connotations. Today, when we think of paganism, we tend to draw associations not only with the ancient polytheism of the Greeks and Romans, but with the druids, witchcraft, occultism, ritual and ceremonial magic, the Jewish Qabalah, and various other schools of thought that do not obviously correlate with one another. In large part, this is due to the efforts of certain nineteenth-century Englishmen who sought to revive ancient spiritual traditions, and who would ultimately synthesize these traditions into something both new and old.

A key touchstone for what we understand as paganism in the modern era starts with the Hermetic Order of the Golden Dawn, a secret society dedicated to the development and promotion of occult ideas. Founded by Wynn Westcott and Samuel MacGregor Mathers, the organization quickly attracted a wide variety of eminent scholars, authors, artists, and poets, including W.B. Yeats, Aleister Crowley, Arthur Machen, and Gerald Gardner. While Crowley would take pleasure in cultivating for himself a reputation of infamy and scandal (while at the same time doing some undeniably insightful work), Gerald Gardner was the one who eventually gave the religion of Wicca to the world, jumpstarting the pagan revival. Wicca incorporated elements of traditional European witchcraft with the secret teachings of the Hermetic Order of the Golden Dawn, which in turn were drawn from the mystic traditions of Judaism, Hinduism, Gnosticism, the religion of ancient Egypt, and the polytheistic traditions of Greece and Rome. At the same time, these British pagans expressed an interest in the lost folk religion of their own island, Druidry, which has accordingly found its way into various schools of modern paganism. This itself is somewhat problematic given that we know almost nothing about what the druids actually believed and practiced. Their culture had no written language, and so the only records we have come from the invading Romans, who are not to be taken as the most reliable and unbiased source when describing the people they were attempting to conquer.

All this is to say that the modern conception of what it means to be a pagan is a more or less hopelessly jumbled mess, and yet there are common threads running throughout all these mingled traditions that allows paganism to have continued meaning for those who follow it. Tracing these threads is one of my core aims in this book, although I feel it is important to be explicit about my use of various terms. In the chapters that follow, I will frequently conflate the word paganism with the traditions of witchcraft, occultism, and ritual magic with which I am familiar. While this may lack some historical authenticity, I do feel that it is an accurate representation of what paganism has become, and how the word is traditionally understood, in the twenty-first century. Other authors, in an attempt to sidestep this difficulty, have sometimes resorted to the word "neo-paganism" to differentiate modern Wiccans and druids from their polytheistic forebears. I, however, find that this form, apart from being unnecessary, is rather ugly and unwieldy, with the prefix "neo-" conferring some sense of blandness or dilution. Modern paganism as I experience it is neither bland nor watered down, instead, being an extremely powerful and life-affirming faith. It is my opinion that context, along with this somewhat lengthy explanatory note, will be sufficient to alleviate any confusion the reader might feel over the various forms of paganism described herein.

For the present, the following definition will suffice: Paganism comprises a loose set of folk beliefs that emphasize a reverence and respect for the natural world, and which may or may not include the worship of gods and the practice of magic.

Varieties of Paganism

As mentioned above, paganism is an umbrella term that encompasses a wide variety of different faiths, and although many of them have elements in common, it is important to be precise in distinguishing different types of pagans. Here are a few of the most common forms of pagan beliefs you're likely to encounter, although since pagan beliefs have existed for thousands of years in every culture of the planet, it is by no means an exhaustive list.

Wicca

Wicca is the most popular form of paganism in the United States and Great Britain. It was formally founded in the 1950s by Gerald Gardner, who claimed to have obtained secret and traditional rites from a coven of witches he met practicing in the New Forest in England. Gardner was also a member of the Hermetic Order of the Golden Dawn, a society founded in the late nineteenth century to explore occultism and metaphysics. The Golden Dawn's practice involved highly formalized rituals drawn from a wide variety of traditions including Egyptian magic, Jewish mysticism, and elements of Greco-Roman mythology. Gardner imported many of the Golden Dawn's practices into Wicca, blending them with the traditions of European witchcraft to create something that was both unique and traditional, ancient and modern. Wicca originally maintained an initiatory structure similar to other magical secret societies, with a focus on group work, covens, and the formal induction of new members based upon certain rites and oaths of secrecy. Nowadays, with the proliferation of readily available information on the internet, any claim to secrecy has become a bit laughable, and most organizations have become less rigid in their approach to recruitment, although you can certainly find groups that still operate within the traditional structure.

Because Wicca comprises the largest pagan community in the English-speaking world, it probably won't be surprising to learn that it has its own various denominations or traditions, some of which are wildly divergent from the others. These range from Gardnerian Wicca, which hews as closely as possible to Gerald Gardner's original instructions, to the more American Anderson Feri Tradition, to Dianic Wicca, Alexandrian Wicca, Raymond Buckland's Seax-Wicca, as well as all-female sects that blend goddess worship with feminism and a number of others that I won't go into here, in part because some of them tend to be quite insular and I don't really know anything about them.

Witches/Witchcraft

Wiccans call themselves witches, but not all witches practice Wicca. The word "witchcraft" describes an informal set of folk traditions practiced by wise women and social outcasts. Essentially witchcraft is any knowledge derived from tradition, experience, and ancient lore that is not adopted and recognized by the more formalized world of science and academia. This can involve natural magic – the use of herbs for healing or other non-culinary applications, animal communication, crystal gazing, reading tea leaves, etc. – as well as more active spellcraft used for finding water, attracting love, and yes, even the occasional curse or hex. For centuries, witchcraft has had a very bad reputation owing to fictional claims about devil worship and Black Masses, in which women were alleged to sell their souls to the devil in exchange for evil powers that would be used to harm the community. There is, of course, no evidence for such hysteria, and the persistence of the fear of witches can be put down to scapegoating, xenophobia, and religious intolerance, helped along by a popular culture that finds endless fascination in the idea of the sinister and malevolent crone. There can be no excuse for this, or for the suffering these attitudes have caused over the centuries to innocent people, but it would be dishonest of me to claim that witches never behave badly. Witches, after all, are just people, and as in any group of people, some are bound to be a bit nasty. So although hexing is a part of some pagans' practice, I do not consider it consistent with or representative of the general set of ethics that underlies the pagan community as a whole. I'll discuss this point in more detail in the next chapter.

Some form of witchcraft or other has been practiced in just about every culture in the world, and while many schools of modern magic lay claim to an ancient lineage, traditional witchcraft probably comes closest to actually earning such a boast, having descended, piecemeal and disorganized, through an oral tradition from who knows when. Through the associations built up over the years and the fact that the word comes from the English language, witchcraft generally refers to traditions originating from Western Europe, which then spread to the Americas. When referring to similar practices in other cultures, you'll often hear words like "shamanism" instead, or else the name of the specific tradition under discussion. While the rites and rituals will obviously be different depending on which culture you look at, the principle of a system of folk beliefs used to cure diseases, bring luck, and communicate with spirits can be recognized as a universal feature of mankind.

Some practitioners of traditional witchcraft resent the fact that the term "witch" has largely become synonymous with Wiccan, especially in the United States, because while the two systems share much in common, there are also many important differences that should not be overlooked, not the least of which is the fact that Wicca has a somewhat formal religious structure totally absent from traditional witchcraft.

Ceremonial Magicians

Ceremonial magic is the art of formalizing and synthesizing a variety of religious and magical traditions from around the world into a modern "scientific" form. I put "scientific" in quotes because there still exists the notion that science is inherently antithetical to anything magical, despite the fact that ceremonial magicians regularly employ the scientific method in their work, controlling for certain variables, repeating experiments, and keeping rigorous records of their successes and failures. Alchemists also fall into this category, as the precursors to modern chemists determined to extract the secrets of the universe from common minerals.

Ceremonial magicians are not necessarily pagans; the medieval grimoires from which they draw much of their materials are firmly rooted in the Judeo-Christian tradition. Still, there tends to be a lot of overlap, not only because magic users like to hang out together, but because modern ceremonial magic draws heavily from pagan ideas and traditions, from the rites of the ancient Egyptians to the mystery religions of the Greeks, to the heresies of the Gnostics and the consciousness-altering techniques of the Hindus and Buddhists.

Ceremonial magicians exist today both as solitary practitioners and in various organizations descended from the Hermetic Order of the Golden Dawn in one way or another, but you're likely to find them hanging around wherever large numbers of pagans are assembled.

Druidry

Druidry was the religion of the Celts in Britain and Ireland before Christianity came to the British Isles. Unfortunately, we know next to nothing about the historical practices of Druidry, as their practitioners didn't write anything down, and we only have small fragments of text from outside observers, the most famous being Julius Caesar, whose account cannot be expected to be entirely reliable. Druidry as it is practiced today is heavily focused on nature and the Earth, eschewing the eclecticism of Wicca for something more specifically Celtic, including a reverence for the traditional gods of Ireland, Scotland, and Wales. Modern druids spend a lot of time out in the forest studying the lore of plants and animals, and getting in touch with the elemental forces that make up the natural world.

Asatru/Heathen

Asatru is a modern take on the religion practiced by ancient Germanic pagans, as depicted in the various Eddas and sagas of the Nordic countries. The extremely rich literary tradition that inspired writers from Wagner to Tolkien with tales of gods and heroes is fertile ground for modern pagans, who honor the old traditions by revering Odin, Freya, and Thor, as well as utilizing Norse and Anglo-Saxon runes for ritual and divinatory purposes. Like the word "pagan", "heathen" was originally a pejorative term that has been reclaimed by the Asatru community to describe themselves, taking pride in the beliefs for which they were historically condemned.

Pagan Reconstructionism

As mentioned under Druidry, we don't know a huge amount about a lot of early pagan traditions, but that hasn't stopped some people from trying to be as faithful to the original religions as they possibly can. Pagan reconstructionists are as much historians and anthropologists as they are spiritual leaders, attempting to use original sources to learn as much as possible about how their faith was actually practiced hundreds or thousands of years ago, and recreate those practices for the modern world. Reconstructionists can be found in Celtic, Norse, and many other traditions from around the world.

Polytheism

Pagan theology can be a bit confusing. In contrast to the Abrahamic religions, most pagan traditions involve some variety of polytheism, the belief in and worship of more than one god. This can take the form of established pantheons from Egypt, Greece, Scandinavia, or Ireland, but it can manifest itself in other forms as well. Wicca, for example, is generally duotheistic, revering a god and a goddess to represent the dual nature of many aspects of the universe. Other pagans leave offerings for a wide variety of domestic or nature deities, not too dissimilar to the folk beliefs in the Faery Folk. It's not uncommon to see modern pagans appealing to a wide variety of gods from different pantheons for different purposes. This can stem from a belief that all gods are really aspects of each other, or that gods are merely symbolic representations of primal forces. Those who stick to a single pantheon usually do so either because of their heritage tying them to a particular location, or just a personal identification with one tradition over the others. It's much more rarely a case of believing that, for example, the Egyptians got it "right" and the Greeks got it "wrong". How each individual decides to work with gods is a matter of personal choice, but to be concise, polytheistic pagans do not confine themselves to the worship of a single deity.

Animism/Pantheism

Not all pagans are polytheistic. While pagan monotheism is rare (though not unknown), pantheism and animism are common alternatives to the belief in many gods. Pantheism is essentially an identification of the deity with the whole of the universe. In other words, pantheism erases the distinction between creator and creation, regarding nature itself as divine. Animism is a similar but distinct philosophy that holds that all objects contain their own spirits, not only animals and plants, but stones, rivers, mountains, houses, and anything else you can think of. Animism is probably the most ancient of religious beliefs and encourages us to have respect for all things, whether animate or not. For those who are interested, my own beliefs tend more towards pantheism with a sprinkling of ceremonial magic than towards any of the other traditions discussed above.

What Is Libertarianism?

Libertarianism is significantly easier to define than paganism. This is partly because it is a modern term, only in common use since about the middle of the twentieth century, and partly because it's far more narrowly focused around a small set of ethical principles. Whereas paganism is vast, global, and has a history that predates writing, libertarianism in the modern context came to be defined in a particular time and place, to fill a particular void.

The word "libertarian" was popularized less than a century ago, but the ideas behind it date back much farther. Previously, those advocating for individual freedom were simply known as "liberals", a perfectly sensible term deriving from the Latin word meaning "free". At some point, however, the term "liberal" came to be associated with the political left, many of whom supported ideas that were anything but liberating, and so a new term, awkward and clunky though it may be, was born out of necessity.

With roots in the philosophy of Aristotle, Hume, Milton, Locke, and Paine, libertarianism really came into its own as an opposition movement to the various forms of totalitarianism that emerged in the twentieth century, from the Third Reich in Germany and the fascists in Italy to Stalinism in Russia and Maoism in China. What all these movements had in common was the brutal suppression of individual liberty and dignity in service to the all-powerful state, a strategy that ultimately led to the deaths of hundreds of millions of people. Even the United

States, founded as a bold experiment in self-government, was not immune from this tendency to centralize power, as the federal government seized control of the economy in order to fight first the Great Depression, then the Nazi Menace, and then the Red Scare. Some saw this as a necessary evil, but others regarded it as becoming the very enemies we claimed to oppose. It was in this environment that so many great anti-authoritarian and libertarian thinkers came to prominence, including the writer George Orwell and the libertarian economists F.A. Hayek and Ludwig von Mises. You will probably notice that economics plays a large role in libertarian thought, and this is partly because some of the philosophy's staunchest advocates have been economists. It's also because the economy consists of nothing more than the productive activities of people, and if you can control those, you can control everything about their lives. Economic policy, more than police or military might, is the lever tyrants use to wield power over an unwilling population.

Libertarians are skeptical of power in all its forms, but especially when it is centralized in one place, with no counterbalancing forces to keep it in check. We believe that people are at their best when they can escape from under the thumb of a master or tyrant, and can take charge of their own destinies. We believe in minding our own business and not interfering with the affairs of others unless we really have to. We believe that personal choice is sacred, and that the freedom to choose is part of what it means to be human.

Broadly speaking, libertarianism is just the idea that, in general, people should be free to pursue happiness in their own way, as long as they aren't hurting anyone else. What this means in practice can vary, as different people have different ideas of what constitutes "hurting", but the basic idea is pretty simple. We all want to be able to make our own choices; libertarianism just asks that you extend that freedom to others as well as to yourself.

Types of Libertarian

Libertarianism as a political philosophy is fairly narrow and specific, dealing only with what constitutes an acceptable use of force in society. As such, it leaves plenty of room for different perspectives and areas of emphasis, leading to many different kinds of libertarians who, while united under a common belief in limited government and personal freedom, may have very different views on everything else, or even what terms like "personal freedom" even mean. Libertarians often joke that the only truly correct libertarian is the one speaking at any given moment, but although the philosophy has at times suffered from excessive gatekeeping and purity tests, for the most part we welcome differences of opinion and celebrate the different types of libertarian thought all sharing the same tent.

Here are just a few of the most common varieties of libertarian you're likely to meet out in the world.

Right Libertarian

A right libertarian is one who approaches the philosophy from the perspective of the political right wing. They are suspicious of government efforts to manage the economy, and tend to emphasize lower taxes, light regulations on business, and the right to bear arms. Right libertarians tend to place more value on traditions such as family, religion, and the nation than their counterparts on the left, although they don't ask or expect the government to maintain or support these things for them.

Left Libertarian

A left libertarian is one who approaches libertarianism from the perspective of the political left wing. They tend to place greater emphasis on civil liberties, privacy rights, freedom of migration, and drug decriminalization. Left libertarians tend to be more cosmopolitan, with greater focus on the international community, technological progress, and the kind of personal autonomy that can lead to accusations of libertinism, in which controversial practices like drug use and prostitution are not only permitted, but celebrated.

Libertarian Anarchist (AKA Anarcho-Capitalist, Voluntarist)

Taken to its logical extreme, the libertarian prohibition on the initiation of force leads to a belief in no government at all, that is to say anarchy. As distinct from the historical use of anarchy which emerged from the communist movement, libertarian anarchists believe that the state is an unnecessary evil, and that society is capable of functioning perfectly well without a single, monopolistic government running the show. Whether or not this is actually true remains to be seen, but a person can dream.

Minarchist

Those who are unconvinced by of the practicality of anarchy are generally minarchists, favoring a minimal state that only exists for certain limited purposes. A minarchist believes that, although the state is necessary to protect individual rights, that protection should be its only function. Thus, police, courts, and the military would be the only responsibilities of government, leaving all other activities to the private sector.

Consequentialist Libertarian

A consequentialist libertarian favors small government and maximum personal liberty because they believe that these things will bring about the best standard of living for society as a whole. This is basically a utilitarian view in which the morality of an action depends solely on its outcome. The consequentialist is not interested in getting bogged down in discussions of political rights, viewing these concepts as overly vague and theoretical. They are only interested in what works. Having observed the failures of governments that grow too large and too powerful, the consequentialist favors a smaller state because they believe such a state will produce a better outcome. They have little use for theory or philosophy.

Deontologist Libertarian

The opposite of the consequentialist, a deontologist favors liberty because they believe it to be a moral imperative. The deontologist believes in doing the right thing, even if the wrong thing can produce better results. By extension, this requires the belief in something like an objective morality that exists independent of particular circumstances. The deontologist is not especially concerned with the ultimate outcomes of his actions, only in doing the morally correct thing at every opportunity. They oppose government action when it involves the violation of rights or the initiation of force against the innocent.

Libertarian Socialist

Long considered to be a contradiction in terms, libertarian socialism is in fact a consistent ideology. The libertarian socialist does not object to the goals of socialism, but merely to the means by which they have historically been achieved, namely, through violence and coercion. The idea of libertarian socialism is to implement the systems of communal property and social responsibility favored by socialists, but only on a strictly voluntary basis. Anyone who wishes to leave the commune must be allowed to do so, or else it ceases to be libertarian and becomes coercive. Of course, many libertarians oppose socialism for other reasons apart from its coercive nature, and so libertarian socialism remains a controversial subset of the movement.

Small L Versus Big L

It's important to distinguish between what are usually called "small l libertarianism" and "big L Libertarianism." In the United States, the third largest political party is the Libertarian

Party, whose platform is based around the philosophy of libertarianism. When you see the word Libertarian spelled with a capital L, it generally refers to the party and its supporters. By contrast, when libertarian is spelled with a lowercase l, it refers to the philosophy of libertarianism and is not associated with any specific political party. This is an important distinction because many libertarians are not Libertarians (and some would argue that plenty of Libertarians are not libertarians.) Some of the more extreme forms of libertarianism shun politics entirely and view voting as an act of aggression that should be avoided, so they object to being lumped in with anyone campaigning for public office.

Chapter 2

The Ethics of Libertarian Paganism

Ethics play a central role in both religion and political philosophy. While the hard sciences strive to give us the what of life, philosophy and religion teach us how we ought to live. Of course, ethics is a complex subject and there is still a great deal of disagreement about what exactly constitutes right and wrong in various circumstances, even after thousands of years of debate. Fortunately, the ethical guidelines proposed by libertarians and pagans alike are fairly straightforward, and complement each other rather well.

I suppose I might as well begin by quoting the passage that first got me thinking about the similarities between ethics in a pagan context and those typically embraced by libertarians. It comes from Penny Billington's *The Path of Druidry*, in a section discussing the wisdom of trying to help people who haven't asked to be helped.

> *[W]ork all you want, but only for yourself. Others, including family members, have the responsibility for their own lives and to work unasked to affect their lives is manipulative. The human need to be altruistic, to want to help, is worthy – in its place. But the key is in the word "need" – our need, feeding our lacks, our need to appear wise and beneficent, perhaps. When we do interfere on a physical level, with advice or actions, it is often rightly seen as controlling: it is frequently tolerated, but rarely welcomed. It is even more bad mannered to attempt to influence events for others on any psychic level, and it is most unethical.*[2]

I found this passage incredibly striking. At that time, I'm afraid to say I had rather stereotypical expectations that the pagan community would be rather hippie-ish, with a somewhat squishy exaltation of altruism and collectivism at the expense of personal responsibility, justice, or even boundaries. Instead, this deep respect for the sovereignty of the individual aligned perfectly with my own views about ethics.

When I first began to attend college, I was advised to read Dale Carnegie's celebrated work, *How to Win Friends and Influence People*, by all accounts a classic and prerequisite for learning how to deal with others. Having been a rather solitary child without many friends, it would seem to have been an appropriate choice. However, I found myself responding to the book with a deep sense of revulsion. I found Carnegie's strategies manipulative and self-serving. The reason to treat people decently is not in order to get them to do something for you, but simply because it's the right thing to do. It turns out I didn't want to "influence people" at all. I wanted them to be free to live their lives any way they choose, without interference or input from me unless it was specifically sought out. Billington's book echoed my sentiments perfectly, and helped me realize that paganism was intrinsically compatible with my preexisting worldview.

It should not be necessary to add that neither pagans nor libertarians are unanimous on ethical questions, and I do not intend to speak on behalf of everyone under either banner, but what follows are a few points that are broadly accepted across the two communities.

Caught NAPping

Libertarians have always been skeptical of the concerted exercise of power and aggression. Instinctively, they are suspicious of any efforts to dominate or coerce others, and as such have always leaned in the direction of political and personal freedom. It took some time to formulate this instinct into a formal code of ethics, but after a few serous attempts to derive a consistent set of libertarian ethics, a handful of authors and philosophers formulated the Non-Aggression Principle, sometimes abbreviated as the NAP. The Non-Aggression Principle simply states that it is ethically impermissible to initiate violence, the threat of violence, or fraud against another person or their property. Once someone has initiated force against you, however, force is permissible in self-defense.

This sounds easy enough and, indeed, may seem like common sense to some people, but when applied consistently, it has some pretty major implications for society as it is currently structured. For example, one of the points libertarians are constantly making is that the outsourcing of violence to a third party does not negate its immorality. We know that murder is wrong, and we don't suspend this judgment if the murderer hires a hit man to do his dirty work for him. In reality, people outsource the threat of violence to agents of the government on a daily basis; for the most part, they just don't realize that's what they're doing.

For example, suppose the city wants to build a new library. To pay for construction, they levy a tax on the citizens and task certain agents with collecting it. Mostly, this goes off without a hitch, but suppose someone doesn't want a new library in town. Suppose he voted against the proposal and refuses to pay the tax, because he disagrees with the use to which his money is being put. In that case, the government agents tasked with collecting the tax will begin to threaten force against the troublemaker. Perhaps they will seize his money against his will, or maybe haul him before a court and threaten to imprison him if he does not comply. If he refuses to leave his home, they may well send men with guns in to extract him. All this because they wish to use his money without his permission.

Libertarians oppose this sort of treatment. They argue that the man has a right to use the money he earns as he wishes, and if the city wishes to build a library, they should raise the money through voluntary donations instead. The oft-heard libertarian slogan "taxation is theft" encapsulates this idea in three words. This may sound like an extreme position, but it is analogous to our hit man example from earlier. If I want to remodel my house, I am obviously not allowed to hold up my neighbor at gunpoint and demand that he cover the cost. That would be theft. A libertarian does not believe that this theft becomes any less wrong just because the person committing it works for the IRS.

The outsourcing of violence to the government happens in all sorts of other ways as well, with the most obvious example being war. Most people have no desire to take guns overseas and use them to shoot at the people who live there, so we hire soldiers to do it on our behalf. It makes us feel better about the whole messy enterprise, and allows us to sleep peacefully at night with no visions of casualties to trouble our dreams. Libertarians do not find killing in the name of war any less reprehensible than killing to settle a personal vendetta against a rival. Except in the very rare cases where a war has to be fought in self-defense (despite what we are told, this almost never happens), killing is equally wrong regardless of whether the killer is in uniform.

Do What Thou Wilt

The Non-Aggression Principle is an idea specific to libertarians, and is not generally known or talked about outside of those circles. In fact, it's often discouraged as a talking point because it is seen as jargon-y, overly narrow, and alienating to people who might otherwise be interested in the philosophy. These objections aside, I still think it is a clear and simple way to explain the basics of libertarian ethics to newcomers. Undoubtedly, most pagans have never heard of the NAP and many would not agree with it. Still, it may be surprising to learn that the ethical code practiced by many modern pagans looks and sounds pretty similar to libertarian thought.

In the early twentieth century, British occultist Aleister Crowley published *The Book of the Law*, a work he claimed he transcribed from a spiritual intelligence called Aiwass. This enigmatic little book contains a lot that is obscure and mysterious, but its central claim, and the one that most influenced pagan thought going forward, was:

> *Do what thou wilt shall be the whole of the Law. Love is the Law, love under will.*

Like much of Crowley's writing, this statement is easily misunderstood by those with only a casual familiarity with his work. At first glance, it appears to say "do whatever you want," but in fact the meaning is more subtle than that. Crowley's use of the word "will" does not refer to idle whims or temptations, but rather to one's true purpose in life. "Do what thou wilt" in this context means something close to "discover your purpose and work to fulfill it." The emphasis on love, often omitted in discussions by Crowley's critics, shows that this ethical guideline is not an endorsement of selfish indulgence or an injunction to disregard the needs of others.

Being rather a big wheel in the pagan community and an acquaintance of Gerald Gardner, founder of the Wiccan religion, Crowley's work had a big influence on the development of paganism in the twentieth century. Another colleague of Gardner's, Doreen Valiente, composed the following couplet to describe her view on Wiccan ethics:

> *Eight words the Wiccan Rede fulfill,*
> *an it harm none, do what ye will.*

This is much closer in meaning to the Non-Aggression Principle than Crowley's original formulation. Do what you like as long as you're not hurting anyone. Again, it sounds reasonable enough.

Note the contrast, however, with the Golden Rule as articulated in the Bible and in numerous other ethical traditions: Do unto others as you would have them do unto you. While the Golden Rule is a positive injunction on how to treat others, the Wiccan Rede is focused on what not to do. Don't hurt others, but apart from that, you're free to live your life as you see fit. We're not going to tell you how to behave; that's something you have to figure out for yourself. This formulation is entirely consistent with libertarian thought, which typically has little interest in prescribing behavior for others apart from condemning certain acts of aggression.

Of course, the question of what constitutes harm is fairly difficult one, and may vary depending on context. The Non-Aggression Principle takes a very narrow view of harm, because it concerns the legitimate use of physical force. Under the Non-Aggression Principle, it is only permissible to use force in self-defense, or the defense of others, from the violent acts or threats of some aggressor. Using force to stop someone from speaking cruelly and insensitively is not permitted, because to do so would be to infringe on the autonomy of the speaker. Note, however, that this does not constitute an endorsement or indifference to non-physical harm. It doesn't say that we should say hurtful things or that it's right to say hurtful things, only that we mustn't hit the person saying them over the head in order to get them to stop. The ethical implication of non-physical forms of harm are surely recognized by almost all libertarians, but they fall outside the scope of the Non-Aggression Principle as originally formulated.

The Wiccan Rede takes a somewhat broader view on the nature of harm, with one particularly nice definition coming from pagan author and artist Robin Wood:

I define 'harm' as interfering with another's free will; lessening someone's freedom of choice; causing unnecessary injury;

damaging someone physically, mentally or spiritually; or wantonly destroying something.[3]

Note the emphasis here on freedom, choice, and personal autonomy. These are all things which are heavily respected in the libertarian community. I think the remainder of the definition is very good as well. Harming others mentally and spiritually is certainly not something we should be doing if we want to live a virtuous and healthy life, nor is wantonly destroying things for no reason, even if it seems like there is no harm in doing so. One of the benefits of an Earth-centered religion like paganism is that it helps us recognize the beauty and value in ordinary things we might otherwise have ignored. To the animist or the pantheist, the smallest pebble is imbued with divinity. Why mar that with destructive actions unless you really need to?

The Rule of Three

The Wiccan Rede is often coupled with a warning about what is known as the Rule of Three, which basically states that any harm you put out into the world will come back to you threefold. This adds some tangible stakes to the Rede, which is thus transformed from a simple suggestion into something more practical. By invoking cosmic retribution, the Rule of Three gives teeth to the Wiccan ethical code, in much the same way that Christian concepts of Heaven and Hell give teeth to the various commandments scattered throughout the Bible. Given this, it should not be surprising to note that many Wiccans do not like the Rule of Three much, and do not subscribe to it.

While many pagans do believe in some sort of karma, it is rarely as simple as "do bad things and bad things will happen to you," and has more to do with how the soul is reincarnated after death, much like in the Hindu or Buddhist faiths. The number three seems here to be fairly arbitrary, and not borne out by any theory or tradition of paganism. Indeed, the Rule of Three is often regarded as no more than a public relations tool to dispel the popular notion that Wiccans are primarily concerned with using dark magic to curse their enemies and bring about mischief.

Of course, the history of witchcraft is filled with embattled and persecuted women and men who did use curses both in self-defense and otherwise. Part of the objection to the Rule of Three is that it seems to forbid not only acts of aggression, but morally justified acts of defense as well. It's also important to remember that not all pagans are Wiccans, and whether or not they choose to subscribe to some version of the Wiccan Rede is up to them. In general, pagans try not to be judgmental or overly prescriptive about moral codes, leaving it up to the individual to decide what constitutes "harm" and whether it is justified in a particular circumstance. Of course, just as some libertarians commit crimes, some pagans will attempt to do harm where it is not warranted. But these exceptions do not invalidate the ethical guidelines that motivate most practitioners.

Minding Your Own Business

One of the cornerstones of libertarian ethics is the idea that people should mind their own business. While not a direct prohibition like the Non-Aggression Principle, this is a general sense that people should be left to tend to their own affairs with minimal interference from outside unless absolutely necessary. There are a couple of reasons for this. The first has to do with the libertarian view on how knowledge is dispersed throughout a society. While other political factions imagine that a few individuals at the top of the hierarchy can amass enough knowledge (to say nothing of wisdom) to make good decisions on behalf of the governed, libertarians view this as a practical impossibility. The United States is made up of about 350 million people, each with their own wants, hopes, and dreams, working in different professions, with different responsibilities, mouths to feed, bills to pay, and different priorities among those various needs and preferences. You're unlikely to have a complete picture of the circumstances of even a close friend whom you've known for decades, so it seems ludicrous to imagine that a politician or bureaucrat in an office building thousands of miles away can do better.

Each individual has what we call the particular knowledge of time and place, ideas related to his circumstances that are generally inaccessible to outsiders. The more such knowledge a person has, the more likely they are to be able to make competent and rational decisions or actions. Anyone attempting to act without the particular knowledge of time and place would be fumbling in the dark, sure to make a mess of things. So, libertarians are usually happy to stand back and let people find their own way without too much interference, recognizing that we may not know as much as the people we would try to help. We can certainly offer assistance and advice, but more than that runs the risk of superimposing our own values and preferences on others with little justification.

Of course, the exception to this is when someone is actively harming others. We have an obligation to step in to protect the weak and innocent. Parents who abuse their children or significant others, thieves, murderers, rapists, arsonists, frauds, and vandals all forfeit their claims to autonomy, but in most other cases the libertarian view is to leave people alone and hope for the best. Some will undoubtedly make bad choices, or at least ones that seem bad from our point of view, but it is not our place to step in unless we are asked to.

Another reason for minding our own business comes from the libertarian respect for personal privacy. This originated largely as a reaction against abuses of power from monarchs and other governmental authorities. In the days when North America was merely a colonial outpost of the British empire, citizens enjoyed no privacy from the prying eyes of the king.

Soldiers could invade private homes and demand to be quartered there; law enforcement could barge in without any due process and rummage through personal papers and effects; and the passage of the Stamp Act, a particularly draconian law designed to extort revenue from the colonists and guard against insurrection, ensured that no one could expect to keep any secrets from the crown.

This lack of privacy inspired the Third and Fourth Amendments to the United States Constitution, preventing soldiers from using private homes and making citizens secure in their private papers and property. If the fledgling government of the United States wanted to invade someone's privacy, they first had to show proof before a court that there was a genuine need to do so.

Today's libertarians see the wisdom in these precautions and remain fiercely protective of privacy rights, a stance that is more important (and more unpopular) than ever in the digital age when computer databases, satellite cameras, and geolocation software built into every phone make it extremely difficult to safeguard your personal information. Of course, millions of people voluntarily surrender their data to social media sites every day for the privilege of looking at pictures of cats and raging over how well all your old classmates seem to be doing on Instagram. If people want to do that, they certainly can. But libertarians remain wary of the implications of mass data collection for personal freedom, keeping an eye on how countries like China have used surveillance to suppress political dissent among their populations. Maintaining an ethos of minding your own business is not only a safeguard against tyranny, it's also just good manners. After all, nobody particularly likes a busybody, do they?

Here again, I think pagans have much in common with libertarians. Perhaps it has something to do with centuries of violent persecution, but there is definitely an appreciation for the importance of privacy in pagan circles. The very word "occult" actually means "hidden," and there is a long tradition of keeping paganism's rites and rituals from the public eye. Secret societies like the Hermetic Order of the Golden Dawn and the Rosicrucians are heavily associated with paganism. These groups would often swear their members to secrecy regarding their practices (although few of these oaths hold up today, and books detailing the minutiae of so-called secret societies are readily available.) In smaller groups, such as the witch coven Gerald Gardner claimed to have contacted, access to knowledge was only granted through an initiation process, usually complete with a secrecy oath as well, and secrets were only shared with those who were deemed worthy after a period of inspection.

Although this level of secrecy may arouse suspicion in non-pagans, contributing to the reputation of paganism as something sinister and wicked, it's easy to understand why it was necessary. For almost two thousand years, people caught worshipping the old gods, practicing magic or witchcraft, and generally failing to conform to Christian orthodoxy could be subject to torture and death. The Inquisition, the Salem Witch Trials, various Holy Wars, and less formalized but no less aggressive hostility towards pagans meant that these activities had to be kept underground. It wasn't until the 1950s that Britain repealed its laws prohibiting witchcraft, and even then "coming out of the broom closet" was not exactly a good way to make friends. In America, the Satanic Panic of the 1970s and 80s imagined demonic rites around every corner, complete with human sacrifices and ritual child abuse. Innocent people were arrested and lives were ruined, in spite of the fact that none of these allegations have stood up to historical scrutiny. Although the secrecy surrounding paganism has lessened in recent years, as tolerance has increased along with more efficient means of electronic communications, it's no wonder that many pagans remain a little timid about openly expressing their faith.

Consent

One of the things libertarians will often say is that they have no wish to prohibit what consenting adults do in their own homes. This is perfectly true, and I'll discuss it further in a bit, but I think that what gets lost in that description is the other side of what it means to consent to something. Consent is a subject that gets a lot of lip service in twenty-first century politics, but there are few who are willing to apply the idea consistently. For example, it is quite correct to insist that sexual contact must only be made with the consent of both parties, and I applaud the accountability that has recently been brought to bear on several prominent men notorious for their harassment, abuse, and assault of women in the workplace. The Me Too movement, as it is broadly called, was unwilling to put up with a status quo in which consent was undervalued or downright ignored, and that can only be a good thing. Yet the importance of consent should not be narrowly restricted to sexual matters. Libertarians believe that consent should be obtained before taking any liberties with another person's body or personal property. Sadly, this view remains, for some reason, in the minority.

To give a few examples of what I'm talking about, let's look at some of the ways in which government agents interfere with the lives of peaceful, law-abiding people without first obtaining consent. The most obvious of these involve the police. The practice of civil asset forfeiture allows police to seize private property if they only suspect someone of a crime. It then remains for the victim to prove himself innocent in court in order to recover his possessions. Obviously, this is a perverse reversal of the principle of "innocent until proven guilty" that is so important to our legal system. Police routinely seize cash, cars, even houses, generally on suspicion of drug-related offenses. Given the costs of appealing these seizures in court, few victims of civil asset forfeiture have the wherewithal or the patience to spend months or years demonstrating their innocence of any wrongdoing. Meanwhile, the police departments are allowed to keep a portion of the seized assets to use as they see fit, creating a very bad incentive for cops. Fortunately, over the last few years more states have been abolishing this practice, but much work remains to be done when legalized theft is allowing law enforcement to just take people's stuff without consent.

There are also plenty of circumstances under which police can invade your privacy and search your person or property without consent. In New York, stop and frisk laws even allowed them to get handsy with passersby whenever they felt like it. And speaking of privacy, thanks to revelations by NSA whistleblower Edward Snowden back in 2013, we now know that the government routinely spies on innocent people, listening to their phone calls and reading their emails without consent. Eminent domain allows government to take your house without consent and give it to wealthy developers anxious to put in another strip mall or freeway. The Thirteenth Amendment to the Constitution prohibits involuntary servitude except as punishment for a crime, but the selective service is still in place, allowing the reinstatement of a draft should Americans ever decide they want to stop fighting in overseas wars. You can even be institutionalized against your will without committing any crimes, as long as some expert is willing to go before a judge and question your sanity. Given all this, that the government doesn't actually engage in sexual assault is somewhat surprising, although anyone who's ever been felt up by a TSA agent may differ with that assessment. Up until a couple of years ago, I wouldn't have believed that the government would be able to ignore the consent of millions of Americans by demanding that they plunge vaccination needles into their arms in order to keep their jobs, eat in a restaurant or go to a movie. Even I underestimated the contempt for bodily autonomy and personal consent held by politicians, bureaucrats, and millions of my fellow citizens.

Libertarians believe that no one, not even a government employee, should be able to take your money, seize your property, compel your labor, physically relocate you, or fondle your special area unless you explicitly consent to it, so long as you're not hurting anyone else. Likewise, we believe that if you and another party do consent to a voluntary agreement, that agreement should be no one else's business. Again, this does not just apply to sex, but to economic matters as well. We see no reason why two people can't negotiate a job, a wage, a housing situation, an exchange of goods, or any other kind of contract without a bureaucrat in an office thousands of miles away dictating which terms are acceptable and which are not. If I offer to work for you for five dollars an hour, and you agree to that price, why should we be prevented from making that mutually acceptable deal? If I want to hire you to give me a haircut even though you don't have a cosmetology license, because I've seen your work and I think you're good, why should I be prohibited from doing so? As long as everyone involved consents, what's the problem? This attitude is why libertarians generally favor legalizing sex work, decriminalizing drugs, and eliminating most labor restrictions that interfere with the voluntary arrangements people choose to make with one another.

Consent is important in the pagan community as well, and with good reason. At a meeting of a pagan book club I attend, a confused stranger once wandered in and asked if we were a cult. We're not, but it's understandable that someone ignorant of the group and of paganism in general might think that. The media prominence of several religious cults, in which charismatic leaders take advantage of hapless followers who want nothing more than a sense of belonging and purpose, means that we have to be especially vigilant to avoid any appearance of impropriety. Even though the vast majority of pagan organizations have nothing in common with these abusive and exploitive organizations, we know that one bad example risks turning us all into media scapegoats. To maintain the integrity of the faith, no pagan should ever put anyone in a position of discomfort or distress, and express consent should always be obtained before doing anything that might infringe on someone's personal boundaries. Pagan seasonal festivals can sometimes involve physical exertion, the use of disorienting sounds, smells, or colors, and alcohol. While not a feature of any ceremony I've ever been a part of, some pagan groups also employ psychotropic substances or nudity. Ethics demands that all participants be informed about what they are about to experience, and freely consent to it, with the option of opting out entirely. Personally, I have never seen these guidelines disrespected, and it's one of the things I truly appreciate about my circle of pagan friends.

The Left-Hand Path

In any discussion of pagan ethics, I feel it necessary to address some of the misconceptions and popular fears surrounding the dark side of paganism. Although acceptance and understanding of what paganism is and what it means has expanded greatly, there are still many who view the religion as an evil one involving Satanism, demon summoning, necromancy, curses, and animal sacrifice. Popular media invariably depicts paganism as "spooky" if not actively dangerous, and the Christians who comprise the dominant demographic in America are taught from a young age that pagans are Hell-bound sinners at best and active servants of darkness at worse.

For the most part, this is all a lot of fuss over nothing. It's true that many pagans, myself included, are attracted to a dark aesthetic, and you probably won't be surprised to learn that there is a substantial overlap between the pagan and Goth communities. But it's at least as common to see pagans outdoors in the sunlight surrounded by flowers and trees than peering into cauldrons through black eyeliner. I've never known anyone who wasn't repulsed by the idea of animal sacrifice, much less practiced it. Pagans are far less likely to try to summon demons than to cast protection spells to keep them out of the house, and while communicating with the dead can be a meaningful part of honoring and reflecting on one's ancestors, it's always done with respect both for the spirits involved and for one's personal safety. Satanism is its own belief system sometimes, though not always, considered a subset of paganism, but it's not at all what you're imagining. I'll address it in a separate section shortly. As I've already mentioned, however, there are some pagans who are not above the occasional curse, and these might be described as followers of Left Hand Path.

In magic, the terms "Right Hand Path" and "Left Hand Path" are used to describe different approaches to the same set of tools, both in terms of goals and methods. Those who follow the Right Hand Path tend to use magic strictly as a means of gaining self-knowledge and knowledge of the divine, with the short-term goal of self-improvement and the long-term goal of spiritual fulfillment and enlightenment. Right Hand Path magicians exalt the spiritual over the material and strive to attain ever higher levels of consciousness in the pursuit of wisdom and inner peace.

Those who follow the Left Hand Path are more interested in using magic to improve their lives and the lives of the people around them in more immediate ways. Spells to attract love, fame, or money are the domain of the Left Hand Path, where the material world is valued over the spiritual one. It's tempting to view the Right Hand Path as "good" and the Left Hand Path as "evil", but it's not as simple as that. Casting spells for personal gain can be ethically problematic, because you never know whether your gain will come at someone else's cost, but there's nothing inherently wrong with living in the material world and wanting to be comfortable in it. You don't have to be an ascetic mystic to be a good person, and in fact one of the lovely things about paganism is its celebration of the physical world as an object of reverence. But pagans understand that there is a dark side to the human personality, and that to ignore that reality is to invite trouble of both a psychological and a spiritual nature.

As in all things, balance is generally the best course. A magician who focuses solely on spiritual development and spends ten hours a day meditating is missing out on a lot of what the world has to offer, and since pagans believe that the world with all its pleasures is imbued with divinity, it seems ungrateful not to partake of its bounty, and to use magic when appropriate as part of that experience. On the other hand, people who devote themselves solely to the Left Hand Path risk losing sight of the bigger picture, and can become petty or even cruel in their pursuit of material gain. This is when you see people starting to employ curses and hexes on their supposed enemies. In many cases, I'm sure that those doing the cursing feel that it is wholly justified and deserved, or that they are only acting in self-defense, and maybe that is the case. I'm not here to judge. But the mechanics of casting an effective curse generally involve raising a huge amount of negativity in the self, and that can hardly be a healthy thing. Those who would risk harm, physical spiritual, or otherwise, to themselves just to inflict harm on someone else have left the path of wisdom, and their actions are not consistent with the ethics of libertarian paganism.

Satanism

While we're on the subject of the darker side of paganism, I ought to address what is often the elephant in the room in any discussion about witchcraft and magic, that old bugaboo Satanism. Thanks to a mountain of urban legends, Hollywood films, and deliberate misinformation many people still think that to practice any form of occult art is synonymous with torturing children, slicing open animals, and worshipping the concept of evil itself. The modern witch hunt that was the Satanic Panic saw innocent lives ruined over the baseless fear that Satanic cults were hiding around every corner, waiting to slip narcotics into your children's Halloween candy and sacrifice young virgins on pentagram altars consecrated to the prince of darkness. Fortunately, a complete lack of evidence for these sorts of activities has allowed the hysteria to die down, but there still exists a prejudicial fear linking paganism and Satanism in the popular mindset.

Let's be clear: Satanists do exist, and they are frequently regarded as a subsect of paganism in the same way as Wicca, but they have almost nothing in common with the monsters you've come to imagine. They don't worship Satan, and they follow a strict moral code that forbids the hurting of children or animals. They are not evil, and in fact all the ones I've met have been pretty nice people. So why all this horrible stereotyping?

The confusion arises from two separate historical phenomena. First is the fact that horned gods, superficially resembling modern depictions of Satan, under a variety of names play a prominent role on Wiccan theology, and have been common in various forms of paganism going back thousands of years, from Pan in Greece to Cernunnos in Britain. Large animal horns linked these gods to the wilderness, to the hunt, and to various forms of masculine energy. While the goddess in Wicca is nurturing and empathetic, the horned god is aloof and untamed. He is wise, but also a trickster, maybe even a bit of a devil. Traditional witch Gemma Gary urges us to embrace this side of his personality, and spend time working with the chaos and mystery of what she calls The Old One. But the horned god of the witches is not evil, and certainly not the supreme antagonist in the universe. Gary clarifies:

Distinct, however, is the witches' 'Devil' from the popular concept of 'Satan' as the very embodiment and actuator of all evil. The Church itself, and the normative society constructed around it, uphold a perverse ideology of moral virtuousness of suffering, poverty and subjugated fear of a terrible, jealous and vengeful god created in their image. The Devil, however, presided over the supposed 'evils' of personal power, freedom, sexual pleasure, dancing, feasting, ecstatic celebration and all things joyous. The witch however, may discern in this figure the 'dark' and 'earthy' half of the divine, divorced and stripped away from Godhead by the Church and given a separate identity.[4]

When Christianity conquered the western world, many of the old gods were relegated to the status of demons, but the various horned gods were folded into the concept of Satan as being fundamentally opposed to the Christian worldview: overly animalistic, hedonistic, and difficult to control. Instead of understanding these undeniably important features of life as legitimate aspects of the divine, they were demonized and classified as sin, the effect of which is that people today regard the horned god as an object of fear rather than one of fascination and reverence.

The second reason why Satanism remains so misunderstood is really the Satanists' own fault. In the 1960s, a rebellious young iconoclast named Anton Szandor LaVey founded The Church of Satan and published *The Satanic Bible* as a vehicle for his personal philosophy. If one bothers to actually read his words, there is nothing remotely sinister about them, but LaVey was the sort of person who took pleasure in provocation, and as he viewed himself in opposition to Christian teachings, he decided to employ the iconography of Satan for the sake of publicity. In a nutshell, LaVey saw Christian dogma as hypocritical and oppressive to the individual, and he felt like rebelling, but what *The Satanic Bible* actually preaches is pretty reasonable, albeit expressed in intentionally inflammatory language. Essentially, LaVey's philosophy celebrates individualism, opposes coercion, and seeks to remove the concept of "sin" from what he views as normal and healthy human appetites for sex, food, and money. That he should latch onto Satan as a symbol is perhaps not surprising, as I've long maintained that the character of Lucifer in John Milton's epic poem *Paradise Lost*, "preferring hard liberty before the yoke of servile pomp"[5], is a fine representation of some very libertarian ideas.

LaVey created further confusion by incorporating some of the ritual techniques of magical societies like the Golden Dawn into his writings. While LaVey probably would have considered himself more of an atheist than a pagan, or even occultist, he found something attractive in the pomp and circumstance surrounding ritual methods, probably not the least of which was that you get to wear cool robes and recite poetry. As a member of the Satanic Temple noted in the 2018 documentary *Hail Satan?* the boring thing about being an atheist is that there is no real iconography that goes along with it. It's simply an absence of belief, and that's something that's hard to represent visually. Part of the fun of Satanism is that adherents get costumes, color schemes, and heavy metal symbols to play around with, which is hardly something you can blame them for.

Today, the Church of Satan exists alongside a number of similar organizations, including the Temple of Satan, which is mainly concerned with preserving the separation of church and state. To my knowledge, none of these groups profess a belief in an actual deity called Satan – if they did, they would be

Christians – and in fact many of them are atheists or agnostics. It seems unjust to accuse people of worshipping a demon when in fact they worship nothing at all, but maybe it's just me.

The eleven rules of conduct published by the Church of Satan are striking in their similarity to libertarian ethics, and include such injunctions as leaving other people alone, minding your own business, not stealing, not making unwanted sexual advances, and not harming innocent people or animals. While I myself do not identify as a Satanist, I can certainly appreciate the sympathies between their individualistic philosophy and my own variety of libertarian paganism.

Chapter 3

Ye Gods, or the Metaphysics of Libertarian Paganism

Perhaps the main thing that distinguishes a religion from other types of personal philosophy is the presence of gods. The first thing we want to know when learning about a new religion is, what are its gods like? How many of them are there? How powerful are they? Are they just or cruel, merciful or vengeful? Are they like humans, filled with pride, envy, and lust? Or are they abstractions, perfect representations of love and light?

With paganism, it's difficult to give simple answers to these questions. As noted above, the word "paganism" in its modern context encompasses an enormous number of different beliefs and practices, and this is nowhere truer than in matters of theology. Having been largely influenced by the folk religions of the ancient Greeks, Romans, Norsemen, Celts and Egyptians, it may come as no surprise to find that polytheism is a common feature of paganism, but even that is not as simple as it appears. There are indeed many who still believe in and worship deities from the Greek or Norse pantheons in a very literal sense. It's not hard to find people who will pray to Odin or to Apollo for help in their various endeavors, and who attempt to develop a personal relationship with these and other gods. Some people confine their worship to one particular pantheon, while others are more eclectic. This eclecticism tends to (but need not necessarily) lead to what's known as "soft polytheism." While hard polytheism is the belief in each god as a separate and distinct entity, soft polytheism regards them as aspects of the same divine force. This can go as far as the belief that all gods are really one god, addressed and invoked differently to appeal to different aspects of the deity. This is not too dissimilar from the Hindu notion that the gods are all aspects of Brahman, the all-encompassing unity of the universe, or the Catholic doctrine of the trinity, in which one god is represented in a threefold form.

Alternatively, some soft polytheists group gods based on their particular dominion. For example, one might regard the Egyptian Thoth and the Greek Hermes as different names for the same being, both being characterized as gods associated with writing, communication, and magic. Similarly, one might group together goddesses of love, gods of war, and trickster deities from diverse pantheons as being essentially the same forces under different aspects or avatars.

Another way of looking at deity is dualistic, with reverence given to a goddess and a god. This is the basic framework established by the Wiccan religion, and has therefore become one of the more popular conceptions of divinity in modern paganism. Again, we can regard this as a more or less pure duotheism, or as a soft polytheism in which all goddesses are aspects of "the" goddess, and all gods are aspects of "the" god. The goddess can then be further subdivided into three archetypes of Maiden, Mother, and Crone, representing the three phases of life. Of course, some people find this dualistic conception of divinity based on gender to be problematic, and some all-female varieties of Wicca have excluded the god altogether. In short, it's complicated.

You may be wondering, do modern pagans really believe that gods like Pan and Thor exist, like, literally? The answer is that, yes, many do, and see it as no odder than the belief in Yahweh or Allah. But like everything else, this is certainly not a unanimous opinion. There are plenty of pagans who think of the gods more metaphorically, as symbolic representations of elemental forces. To the more psychologically minded, the gods may serve as symbols that we invoke to trigger something within ourselves rather than objective external entities. Others reject polytheism entirely in favor of a different conception of the divine. Pantheists regard all of creation as part of, or identical with, god, while animists believe that everything, not just animals and plants, but rocks and manufactured objects, has an independent spirit within. There is even a movement of atheistic pagans who don't believe in any sort of god, so like I said, it's complicated.

Monotheism and Authority

Perhaps the rarest, though certainly not unheard of, conception of divinity in pagan circles is one that mirrors the omnipotent, omniscient, interventionist, monotheistic god of religions like Judaism, Christianity, and Islam. I think the reason for this is part of what makes paganism appealing to me as a libertarian: skepticism towards authority.

Before I discovered paganism, I spent a long time trying to read about and understand Christianity. As the dominant faith in the country in which I was raised, I wanted to make a concerted effort to see what all the fuss was about, and whether I too might find my way towards becoming a Christian. I read the Bible from cover to cover (something I was dismayed to find few of the Christians I knew had done), attended church services, and read the works of prominent theologians and apologists. And I would say that this was not an unprofitable study. The Bible is filled with many great stories and much wisdom; churches can be beautiful and inspiring; and G.K. Chesterton remains one of my favorite writers and thinkers, although he ultimately failed to convert me to Catholicism. But throughout all of this, I could never escape the one thing that really troubled me, and that was that Yahweh seemed to be a bit of a bully.

I'm not even talking about the divinely-sanctioned cruelty and genocide so prevalent throughout the Old Testament, although to be sure that also gave me considerable pause. More fundamental is the idea that we are all ruled by, as the noted atheist Christopher Hitchens often put it, a celestial dictator, who makes demands of us and threatens disobedience with eternal punishment.

Mircea Eliade, in his exhaustively researched *The History of Religious Ideas*, illustrates my difficulty here in a rare moment of editorializing:

> *Yahweh's anthropomorphism has a twofold aspect. On the one hand, Yahweh displays qualities and faults that are specifically human: compassion and hate, joy and grief, forgiveness and vengeance. (However, he does not show the weaknesses and faults of the Homeric gods, and he will not tolerate being ridiculed, as certain Olympians do.) On the other hand, unlike the majority of divinities, Yahweh does not reflect the human situation; he does not have a family, but only a celestial court: Yahweh is alone. Are we to see another anthropomorphic characteristic in the fact that he demands absolute obedience from his worshippers, like an Oriental despot? This seems rather to be an inhuman desire for absolute perfection and purity The intolerance and fanaticism that are characteristic of the prophets and missionaries of the three monotheisms have their model and their justification in Yahweh's example.*[6]

It is this very "demand for absolute obedience" that seems to me disagreeable coming from a being elsewhere described as being composed of pure love. That is certainly not how I treat the people I love, and if I did, I can imagine how they would react. Not with worship, I can tell you that.

We are often told that we derive our morals from religion, and that an atheistic society would be one without a conscience, but the paradox of Christian morality is that being good purely out of fear of punishment is no virtue at all. Goodness must be freely chosen without coercion to be in any sense meaningful. But coercion seems to be the principal business of the god of the Bible, and business is good indeed. Even when he doesn't directly intervene in human affairs to enforce his will via a flood or the destruction of a perfectly nice tower, the threat of eternal damnation lies behind every "thou shalt not." When I bring up these objections, Christians are quick to point out that the teachings of the New Testament relieve us of the numerous injunctions spelled out in Exodus and Leviticus. Fair enough, but these are replaced by yet another form of coercion: accept and love Jesus Christ, or else. We are repeatedly told that it is only through Christ that salvation is possible. In other words, you can be the kindest, most generous, and indeed holy person who ever walked the Earth, but if you don't pay lip service to the big guy, it's all in vain. We are commanded to worship, and that's just not a command I can get behind.

The same impulse that makes me bristle at being told I have to say the Pledge of Allegiance whether I want to or not causes me to reject any demand – divine or otherwise – for blind, unquestioning obedience and loyalty. The same logic that makes me object to the occupant of the White House telling me what to do with my life and my body makes me no more sympathetic to similar orders issuing from behind the Pearly Gates. I'll make my own decisions, thanks.

Now, I really don't mean to pick on Christians. That's not what this book is about. I'm simply trying to give an explanation of why Christianity doesn't work for me, and the ways in which it conflicts with my essential libertarian views. There are plenty of Christian libertarians. There are even some Christian pagans. More power to them. But I can't personally reconcile the two belief systems. Monotheism has always just seemed a little too authoritarian to my liking.

So then, you may be wondering, why not atheism? Surely us liberty types are all about rationality and empiricism, right? Wasn't Ayn Rand a famously fervent atheist? Where do you get off bringing gods and mysticism into a philosophy rooted in such earthly pursuits as economics and political science? These are good questions, and I'll do my best to answer them.

To be sure, there are plenty of atheist libertarians. As mentioned, Ayn Rand's philosophy of Objectivism was explicitly atheist, although it's worth noting that Rand didn't consider herself a libertarian and in fact was highly critical of them. There are also plenty of strands of strict rationalism within libertarian economics, and one certainly doesn't require any variety of mysticism or religion to be a libertarian. That being said, two of the key features of libertarian thought are a certain intellectual humility, and the recognition that people are different and should be free to pursue happiness in different ways. Libertarianism is no more a monolith than paganism is, so while there is no shortage of materialism in libertarian circles, there are also those who hunger for spirituality and something beyond the purely physical. For those who object to the emphasis on obedience in Abrahamic religions, paganism offers a way to explore the spiritual side of life that is more pluralistic and decentralized.

The Morality of Choice

The importance of choice is one of the key features of libertarian thought, so much so that *Free to Choose* was the title of both an influential book and television series by celebrated libertarian economist Milton Friedman. The ability of individuals to make decisions about their own lives is crucial not only because they are generally the ones most competent to do so, but for deeper moral reasons as well. The objection to authoritarian policies is that they rob people of their freedom to choose, replacing it with a choice made by a politician, a bureaucrat, or a scientist. We may judge these choices to be either good or bad, but that is largely beside the point. You ought to have the power to shape your life and pursue happiness in your own way, even if that creates the risk of disastrous failure. It's no one else's responsibility, no matter how wise or well-intentioned they may seem.

The freedom to choose also has some pretty profound implications for morality and theology. Something that has always bothered me about Christianity is the simultaneous claim that god gave humans free will, but that he will punish us for eternity if we use it in ways of which he disapproves. Can a choice really be said to be free if it is coerced? I'm reminded of the responses I sometimes get from non-libertarians when I complain about, for example, laws prohibiting the use of certain drugs. Why shouldn't I be free to choose what I put in my body? To this, some people will trenchantly reply that I do have that choice: I can choose to follow the law or choose to go to jail. If we take this attitude, it's clear that the idea of freedom to choose loses most if not all of its meaning (and I'm quick to note that the argument evaporates when I apply the same logic to laws my interlocutor doesn't like).

The nature of virtue is that it must be freely chosen; it cannot be compelled. The person who refrains from evil purely out of terror for his own safety is no more moral that a robot following its programming or a small animal responding to basic stimuli. The virtuous person has to have the option not only to do bad things, but to get away with them, and yet choose the good anyway. This is a big part of the thesis of Anthony Burgess's novel *A Clockwork Orange*, and its iconic film adaptation by Stanley Kubrick. The protagonist, Alex, is a reprehensible teen hooligan who engages in assault and rape for kicks, until he is apprehended and subjected to an experimental therapy alleged to "cure" criminal behavior. Alex is psychologically conditioned to become physically ill to the point of incapacitation whenever he contemplates an act of violence. He is therefore unable to commit further crimes, but his mind is unchanged. He still wishes to do evil, he is just overcome with pain and sickness when he attempts it. In the New Testament, Jesus cautions that sinning in your heart is equivalent to actually committing a wicked act, and that point would seem to be borne out here.

But the Bible is inconsistent here, as it is on so many issues. We are told both that what matters is not what we do, but how we feel, and that our actions are constrained by the constant threat of hellfire. Under these conditions, I would argue that true virtue is virtually impossible to achieve, since god has offered a powerful incentive that will certainly affect our freedom of choice. If anyone truly believes in the reality of Hell, there's no way that his choice to do good can be made independent of that belief, and it becomes impossible to tell how much of his behavior, or even his inner feelings, are motivated by avoiding damnation rather than for their own sake. Virtues is doing the right thing when no one is watching, and as Christians are always quick to tell us, god is always watching. We can observe apparently virtuous behavior on the part of the believer, but the threat of eternal damnation rather taints the sincerity of his motives.

Paganism makes no such threat. One of the amusing inaccuracies of how paganism is portrayed in the media is the constant insistence that pagans worship Satan and seek to do his bidding. Satan is a Christian concept, which does not exist in paganism. There is no supreme source of evil in pagan theology, in which the gods are more complex than simply the embodiment of good and bad. There is certainly no belief in a realm of eternal torment to which the wicked are banished after death. While pagans do have a code of ethics, this code is not enforced by threats or coercion. Earlier, I mentioned that the Rule of Three espoused by some sects of paganism is controversial, and here is another reason why. The Rule of Three, stating that any evil you do will return to you threefold, allows the individual to abdicate a certain degree of responsibility for their actions. Like the god-fearing Christian, the believer in the Rule of Three can lean on the fear of negative consequences as a justification for refraining from evil. The rest of us have no such crutch. The moral consequences of what we do on Earth rests on us alone, and we have to live with what we do. True freedom of choice is a heavy responsibility, which requires lots of introspection and soul searching. It's less about the fear of consequences, and more about the kind of life we've decided we want to live.

It is true that permitting individuals the choice to do evil without consequence can result in some bad outcomes, but it's also the only way we can be sure that the good is coming from a place of honest principle rather than mere expediency. This is why libertarians argue that you can't and shouldn't legislate morality. We accept that legal prohibitions against violence and theft are good and proper, but when it comes to more abstract notions of good and evil, it's better to leave the choice up to the individual. If you want people to be good, you have to persuade them, you can't force them. In this vein, libertarians have argued against laws prohibiting hate speech or bigotry. You can't legislate bad people out of existence, but you can drive them underground. Better to let them reveal themselves through their speech and actions so we know who they are and can avoid them, than to create a class of secret bigots with hate in their hearts but a congenial smile on their lips.

Gods à la Carte

Noted libertarian author and organizer Matt Kibbe has often pointed out that the tremendous tendency for young people to want to curate every aspect of their lives, from the music they listen to and the clothes they wear to the political views and philosophies they adopt, is a fundamentally libertarian impulse. Why should anyone be forced to pay for a complete cable package when you only care about a couple of channels? Why should your money go to support the Home Shopping Network when all you really want to watch is ESPN? If you can pick your entertainment, it only makes sense that you should be able to pick your beliefs, without being dragged into a bunch of dogmatic traditions that have no relevance to your life or the things you care about.

Paganism in its modern form can be described as an a la carte religion. While I'm sure some who follow a specific traditional path will take offense at this, it's nevertheless quite common for practicing pagans to do a bit of picking and choosing about which elements of ancient cultures they follow and which they don't. For example, many texts on witchcraft and magic from the Renaissance period recommend animal sacrifice for certain rituals. While elements of these rituals survive today, I don't know anyone who would even consider hurting an animal as part of a magical act; indeed, the very idea is antithetical to the kind of spiritual life the pagans I know are striving for. Yet they see no problem in taking the good ideas from the past while leaving the bad ones in the dust where they belong.

Similarly, pagans tend to pick and choose the deities and pantheons with which they identify and interact, rarely being afraid to mix and match. A witch of Celtic descent might set up an altar to Brigid, while at the same time praying to the Greek moon goddess Selene during lunar ceremonies, or appealing to the Egyptian Thoth for advice on matters of writing, communication, and spellcraft. This eclecticism stands in contrast with the dogmas of the monotheistic religions, whose adherents are generally expected to believe everything in their sacred texts, even the inconvenient, outdated, and downright unpleasant stuff. You might hear someone denounced as "not a real Catholic" if they support abortion rights, or "not a real Muslim" if they drink alcohol, but you will rarely hear the same accusation leveled at pagans, who generally frown on gatekeeping. Anyone who claimed that you can't be a real pagan unless you believe in Osiris would be regarded, at least in my circles, as fairly silly, and would probably not get invited to many parties.

In this sense, paganism is a religion that values individual choice and customization, traits also highly prized by libertarians.

Chapter 4

Politics and Religion

Render under Caesar what is Caesar's, and render unto God what is God's.[7] You may recall this Biblical quotation as an injunction to separate the worldly business of politics from more spiritual matters. Perhaps that is good advice, but the fact is that politics and religion have always been bound together. Throughout most of history, the head of state and the high priest of a country's dominant religion were generally the same person. Since the pharaohs of ancient Egypt, kings have asserted their divine right to rule, and divine sanction for the decisions they make while on the throne.

Even in more recent years when the concept of separation of church and state is more widespread, politics has a lot to do with how religions are practiced. There are still plenty of theocracies around the globe, but no nation is immune from political forces becoming mingled with metaphysical ones. There's a reason for this. Both politics and religion involve deeply held beliefs about how the world works and how we should live our lives. Politics is, at its heart, philosophy. Religion is just philosophy with gods attached. It's no wonder that the two subjects can be so divisive, and why traditional wisdom holds that neither should be discussed around the dinner table if you want to keep your relationships with friends and family intact.

Personally, I prefer to keep my spiritual practice separate from any political activities, and I resist any temptation to allow politics to taint the relationships or activities I have with my pagan friends and acquaintances. This is in part because the modern pagan movement is fiercely diverse and resistant to categorization, especially when it comes to political beliefs. Author and journalist Margot Adler pointed this out in her comprehensive survey of American paganism, *Drawing Down the Moon*:

> *In the 1970s, when I asked one hundred Pagans to list their political positions, the assortment was astonishing. There were old-style conservatives and liberals, a scattering of Democrats and Republicans, twenty different styles of anarchists (ranging from Ayn Randists to leftist revolutionaries), many libertarians, a couple of Marxists, and one Fascist.*[8]

She goes on to point out that there is broad disagreement about whether paganism is itself political, and even what is meant by the term "politics". It seems to me that this is as true now as it was when she wrote it, and it would be foolish to try to pigeonhole contemporary pagans by trying to ascribe to them any particular political position.

Still, there are some issues which I feel transcend partisanship, and whose underlying principles are deeply ingrained in both the philosophy of libertarianism and the pagan worldview, as diverse as that has proven to be. As I said in the Introduction, this is not about telling anyone how they ought to feel about any political issue, and especially any specific legislation or candidate. Instead, I want to look at a couple of broad political principles where I feel that pagans and libertarians can find some common ground.

A Libertarian Approach to Religion

One might be tempted to ask, if one were to design a religion from the ground up based on libertarian principles, what would such a religion look like? Perhaps the best, but least satisfying answer would be that libertarians would never want to design something as complex and nuanced as religion in the first place. Better to let beliefs and practices emerge organically through the actions of individuals employing their own particular knowledge of time and place. Institutions which are centrally designed and managed tend never to work as well as those which employ the combined knowledge and experience of millions, working in a decentralized fashion.

In a sense, this could be said to be true of all religions (with the possible exception of Scientology) but there seems something particularly appropriate about this description as it applies to paganism. It could be argued that Wicca has a designer in the form of Gerald Gardner, but Wicca does not represent all of paganism, and even Gardner was influenced by a huge variety of traditions cobbled together from various sources, so that you could say that Wicca was merely assembled rather than designed. Nor did Gardner try to hold onto the reins of Wicca after its introduction, allowing it to flourish and diversify into a wide variety of separate practices created by individuals to suit their various needs. Other varieties of paganism are even more loosely assembled, collecting the folk traditions built up over hundreds or thousands of years and somehow collecting them into a workable modern faith. The whole thing is very decentralized and spontaneous, just the way libertarians like it.

But there is another aspect of paganism which I think sets it apart from other religions, and allows its adherents to embrace a do-it-yourself spirit absent from churches with more rigid historical or dogmatic structures. It's something that has been used to criticize pagans over the years, but which I actually think is a strength rather than a weakness. One could argue that the pagan revival kicked off in earnest in 1921, with the publication of Margaret Murray's *The Witch-Cult in Western Europe*. Murray was an anthropologist and Egyptologist who claimed that modern witchcraft was the product of an unbroken, centuries-old tradition carried on by groups of women operating in secret and passing their knowledge down through the ages via oral tradition. Murray's work drew heavily from books such as James Frazer's *The Golden Bough*, a massively influential work of questionable scholarship on ancient religious traditions, and Charles Godfrey Leland's *Aradia: The Gospel of the Witches*, which the author represented as coming directly from one of these hereditary witches in Italy. The idea that modern witches were carrying on a pre-Christian tradition that had survived in secret for all this time was appealing to many, who felt it added both legitimacy and mystique to their practice.

As the twentieth century advanced and scholarship improved, Murray's claims, along with Leland's and much of Frazer's work, came to be pretty conclusively debunked. There was no evidence for this ancient witch cult, and while many folk traditions still used by paganism are indeed old, there's no reason to believe that things like the ritual structure of Wicca bear any resemblance to what pre-Christian pagans would have done. Some pagans took umbrage at what they saw as an effort to delegitimize their faith, and indeed you can still find many modern books on Wicca that perpetuate the fictions of Murray and Leland. But for the most part, modern pagans have come to accept that the major part of their traditions were invented in the nineteenth and twentieth centuries by people like Gerald Gardner, Aleister Crowley, Doreen Valiente, and other influential pagans and occultists. And you know what? That's totally fine.

In a way, the fact that pagans lack a consistent historical basis for their practice is freeing. We don't need to worry about whether what we're doing is legitimate or valid (whatever those words mean in this context), but only whether it provides meaning and transcendent experiences to people's lives. Not being tied to the idea that we're replicating the rituals of the past means we are free to be inventive, creating or adapting various elements of worship to suit our own needs and the needs of those around us. Since no one is in a position of authority to tell us what paganism really is, the religion can be developed and improved through the collective action of all its adherents.

There are those who would argue that the debunking of various historical claims means that paganism is "fake" and not to be taken seriously. This is an unfortunate attitude that misunderstands the role of spiritual practice in the life of an individual. There is nothing particularly sacred about that which is old. I wouldn't want to place my life in the hands of a surgeon who practiced ancient techniques while neglecting modern advances. What matters is what gives meaning to people, and modern paganism certainly does that. In my view, the collaborative process of continual invention and adaptation which defines modern paganism is one of the things that makes it so vibrant and appealing, as well as being a particularly libertarian approach to religion.

Freedom of Religion

For several thousand years, starting from the dawn of Christianity and lasting until present day, when it's still regarded by many people as a bit fringe and weird, paganism was not a mainstream religion. Despite the near universality of pagan practices all around the globe dating back into prehistory, the rise of monotheism and, more specifically, the idea that there was such a thing as a "one true faith" meant that those who wished to worship the old gods had to do so more or less in secret. Those who went public with their beliefs risked not only persecution and ridicule, but sometimes death.

The Bible commands the Israelites to pillage and murder their neighboring tribes who worship gods from other traditions, gods which would later be recast as demons in the development of the Christian study of demonology. Poring through the list of the supposed Chieftains of Hell yields names that will be familiar to the student of comparative anthropology, names like Marduk and Baal, the nearly forgotten deities of ancient Middle Eastern tribes.

In the Middle Ages, the Inquisition, under directives from the Catholic Church, sought out and punished heretics, a heretic being anyone who refused to conform to the Church's teachings about divinity. Pagans, with their belief in and devotion to multiple gods, certainly fell into that category. After all, the very first of the Ten Commandments demands "thou shalt have no other gods before me." It's an interesting, albeit tangential, point that the text never claims that no other gods exist, only that it's a sin to worship them.

During this time period, the influential philosopher Baruch Spinoza developed his concept of "pantheism", the idea that divinity exists in the entire universe, and that the distinction between creator and creation is largely an artificial and meaningless one. Pantheism is an important aspect of pagan thought, as pagans tend to see god in every tree, flower, and stone, as well as in the stars and planets of the night sky. Unfortunately, the environment in which Spinoza was writing was not one which would tolerate such unconventional thinking, and as a result his published works tend to use language which is obscure to the point of incomprehensibility. Unable to state his views openly, Spinoza had to use strangled philosophical and theological jargon to avoid charges of heresy, which had the side effect of making his work fairly inaccessible to those who might have otherwise benefited from his insights.

In perhaps the most famous case of religious persecution against pagans, the Salem Witch Trials in seventeenth century Massachusetts resulted in multiple deaths of innocent people, most of whom were probably not even pagans. They were just bystanders who got caught up in a wave of anti-pagan paranoia and mob justice.

In Britain, laws prohibiting witchcraft remained on the books until the 1950s. Although these laws were seldom actually enforced, the fact that they took so long to repeal is pretty shocking, especially given that their existence deterred neo-pagan thought leaders like Gerald Gardner from writing openly about their experiences. Gardner's first book was published under a pseudonym, and was presented as fiction in order to avoid punishment from the authorities.

It's unclear to what extent the decline in the persecution of pagans is due to increased religious tolerance rather than a simple decline in the belief in the efficacy of magic and witchcraft. The Catholic apologist and gifted writer G.K. Chesterton, whose work I generally admire immensely, once lamentably remarked that the reason we no longer burn witches is that we don't believe in them, not that they don't deserve to be burnt.

Given that persecution for their beliefs has been a longstanding reality for pagans for thousands of years, it is only natural that they would tend to value the freedom of religion, a legal guarantee that no one will be punished for worshipping the wrong god, praying the wrong way, or using the wrong ceremonial props or structure. This is something on which libertarians also place great importance.

The men who drafted the United States Constitution were not exactly religious fundamentalists. While cagey about the precise nature of their beliefs, the founders give every appearance of having been a mixture of agnostics, deists, and possibly even a couple of atheists rather than the dyed in the wool Christians they are sometimes represented as. Thomas Jefferson even famously mutilated his copy of the Bible to highlight the parts he found important and meaningful, and discarding those he found offensive and objectionable.

When it came time to draft a Bill of Rights for the Constitution, therefore, religious liberty was high on the list of priorities. The fact that the First Amendment guarantees not only freedom of speech and of the press, but also religious liberty, is no accident. The founders had seen the tyranny that could result from too close a marriage between church and state.

Today, libertarians continue to champion the freedom for individuals to worship as they please, rejecting claims that the United States is "a Christian nation," but instead one which is also full of Jews, Hindus, Muslims, atheists and, of course, pagans.

Privacy

Privacy rights go hand in hand with freedom of religion, and are important for many of the same reasons. Part of living your life in peace and quiet requires that other people not be too nosy about what you're up to, especially if they intend to persecute you for what you do in your own home. Just as you have the right to worship any way you want, you have the right to do so in privacy, without the neighbors concerning themselves with your private spiritual practice. Since persecution is something pagans know a thing or two about, privacy remains an especially important part of the tradition for many people. Even though witches and heretics are no longer killed or tortured for their views in most parts of the world, paganism can still carry a stigma for those who don't understand it. The mass hysteria of the Satanic Panic is still only a few decades in the past, and a lot of people still associate paganism and its accompanying symbols with devil worship, child abuse, wild orgies, and ritual sacrifice. This means that going around talking about your religion has the potential to be dangerous – not in the burning at the stake kind of way, but in terms of maintaining social and professional relationships. Of course, some people like the attention and others even revel in a certain amount of shock value that comes from telling people you practice magic and hold rituals at the full moon, but that's not for everyone, and it's important that those who wish to remain anonymous can do so without being driven "out of the broom closet," as some like to say.

Privacy is an extremely important issue for libertarians as well. As technology has improved and we have all become more interconnected, it has become harder and harder to retain a degree of personal privacy either from corporate data collectors or government surveillance agencies. Our phones contain global positioning software that allow our every movement to be tracked; the websites we use collect data about our browsing and spending habits; satellites take photos of our homes and can identify us with facial recognition software; the police are given broad authority to search our vehicles or our persons at will. Electronic encryption, which is what makes it possible to make a credit card purchase online without having your identity stolen, is under continual assault from governments who resent the fact that someone might be able to do something they don't know about.

In 2013, Edward Snowden, then an employee of the National Security Administration, was forced to flee the country when he revealed that the agency was engaged in mass, warrantless spying on innocent Americans in violation of the law, the Constitution, and the basic rules of human decency. Among the creepier revelations from that case was the admission that some of the agency's staff had used their power to spy on current and former romantic partners.

Libertarians are appalled by all of this because they understand that knowledge is power, and that the potential for the data collected from mass surveillance to be abused is astronomical. Dystopian writers like George Orwell have long used the image of total surveillance to warn against the dangers of a too-powerful state, with ominous expressions like "Big Brother Is Watching", but we need not turn to fiction to understand what can happen when the citizenry is held under a microscope. The totalitarian regimes of the twentieth century, from Germany, to the Soviet Union, to China, all regarded privacy as a threat to their power, and did whatever they could to stamp it out. It's hard to resist a tyrannical regime if the people in charge know every word you say or think.

Rationalism and Scientism

On the whole, libertarian personalities tend towards the analytical, logical, left-brained sorts, exactly the type you might expect to embrace rationalism, the worship of reason as an instrument capable of solving all of life's mysteries. Indeed, several prominent libertarian thinkers have been overtly critical of anything smacking of mysticism. Ayn Rand was extremely hostile towards religion as an abdication of man's ability to think, and economist Murray Rothbard criticized F.A. Hayek's concept of spontaneous order as overly metaphysical. There was nothing spontaneous, he argued, in the deliberate and reasoned choices of individuals which make up the order we see in society. Nevertheless, these attitudes, at least in my opinion, neglect the core principles underlying the belief in individual freedom, for even these strident defenders of rationalism were perfectly aware of the danger of the philosophy when taken to its logical extreme.

We can gain some insight into this apparent paradox by taking a brief diversion into the world of Tarot, the elaborately illustrated, 78-card deck often used by occultists and pagans for spiritual insight into the subconscious. While tarot cards have been around for centuries, a consistent art of reading their symbols has only been finely developed in the last century or so, starting with images produced by the Hermetic Order of the Golden Dawn, and introduced to the public by the combined efforts of occultist Arthur Edward Waite and artist Pamela Coleman Smith. This deck, known as the Rider-Waite-Smith deck after its publisher, author, and illustrator respectively, remains the most popular set of tarot cards to this day, and for good reason. Waite took considerable care to ensure that each card carried an illustration that conveyed, or at least hinted at, its occult significance.

Among the innovations applied to this pack of fortune telling cards was an elaborate system of correspondences that mapped every card in the deck onto various concepts of the astrology, the classical elements, aspects of human personality, and the Hebrew alphabet (this latter contribution being owed to the nineteenth century French occultist Eliphas Levi.) Like modern playing cards, the tarot contains four suits, indicated by wands, cups, swords, and pentacles, with each suit corresponding both to an element and a facet of personality. Reason, represented by the element Air, corresponds to the suit of swords, whose members are generally interpreted as somewhat violent and disruptive. For example, the last two cards in the suit, the nine and ten of swords, are called, respectively, "Despair, or Cruelty" and "Ruin".

At first glance, this is somewhat puzzling. The nines in the other suits are generally positive and balanced cards, representing their respective elements in their most balanced and favorable positions, whereas the tens represent the element in its most undiluted form. Why should reason, which we generally regard as a virtue, turn so sour in its representation in the tarot? It's no secret that reason and mysticism have long been enemies, and not only because of the lack of scientific support for metaphysical phenomena. Anyone who has tried meditating for any period of time can answer this mystery with ease. The rational mind is violently resistant to the meditator's efforts to bring it under control, to silence thought for the purposes of spiritual reflection. As soon as we try to quiet the mind, it rebels like a cornered animal, bombarding our brains with an avalanche of urgent thoughts and questions, shattering our attempts at inner peace. Like a petulant child, the mind demands attention at all times, and throws a tantrum whenever that attention is withheld, even for the briefest of moments. The grueling process of acquiring discipline over one's own thoughts is perhaps the greatest obstacle faced by the aspiring magic-user, as without this discipline any attempts to commune with the divine or access the hidden powers of one's own subconscious are quite impossible. It is only through long and arduous practice that we can bring the rambunctious mind under control and make any real progress in meditation.

This phenomenon, well understood by students of the esoteric, can partially explain the tarot's attitude towards reason, but not wholly. There is more going on. In his often obscure treatise on tarot, *The Book of Thoth*, Aleister Crowley describes the ten of swords as "reason gone mad". Crowley's own contributions to the development of the tarot are considerable, and his opinions should not be disregarded lightly. The madness he refers to is what happens when you exalt reason above all other considerations, abandoning such human traits as mercy or compassion. The "cruelty" of the nine of swords is that of the hanging judge so zealous in the rigid application of the law that he makes no allowances for extenuating circumstances or the possibility of rehabilitation, remorse, or reform. Likewise, the "ruin" in the ten of swords carries this same concept to the society-wide level. Remember that Crowley lived through the first half of the twentieth century, witnessing the horrors of the Bolsheviks, the American eugenics movement, and the rise of Nazism. All of these authoritarian regimes had in common the idea that science, centrally administered from a position of government authority, could build a better world without having to bother with pesky little things like human nature or individual rights.

The theory behind communist regimes in Russia, China, and Cambodia was that a central government could do away with the messy business of markets and prices, and run everything on a scientific basis through a government bureaucracy. This overwhelmingly misplaced faith in scientific experts to extend their narrow expertise into restructuring entire societies is known as "scientism". It's an idea which has resulted in the deaths of millions, and which libertarian economists and political theorists from Ludwig von Mises to Karl Popper have devoted many volumes to debunking. Given Crowley's position in the front row seat of history, it's not hard to imagine why he would associate unrestrained rationalism with "ruin" and with "reason gone mad."

Despite the undisputable failures of rationalism in the twentieth century, there remains a certain class of political leaders who remain steadfastly devoted to the idea of expert-ocracy. Fortunately, a healthy skepticism towards rationalism is an area on which pagans and libertarians can find common ground.

Chapter 5

Magic and Markets

What's All This Magic Business, Anyway?

It's no secret that magic and witchcraft play a significant role in many forms of modern paganism. This fact has not only resulted in some nasty persecution over the years in the form of witch hunts and heresy trials, but it continues to serve as a source of mockery for those who dislike or misunderstand pagan beliefs. With this in mind, we would do well to define some terms before proceeding further.

First of all, it's worth pointing out that a belief in something resembling magic is not unique to paganism. Catholics regularly participate in a rite in which bread and wine are believed to literally transform into the flesh and blood of Jesus Christ, and all religions believe in some version of the power of prayer. Buddhists and Hindus believe that apparently miraculous abilities are accessible through meditation and an altering of ordinary consciousness. Atheists and materialists may scoff at all of these beliefs as equally ridiculous, but anyone who professes a religion should think twice before singling out pagans as particularly credulous.

Having said that, I think that there's a huge amount of misunderstanding around the idea of magic and witchcraft, at least as they are understood by modern pagans. The word "magic" evokes the flashy illusions of stage magicians, in which lovely assistants are sawn in half without harm, made to levitate, or vanish entirely. The magician snaps his fingers, and hey presto! Something seemingly impossible happens. This association led to Aleister Crowley employing the spelling "magick" in order to distinguish his art from mere parlor tricks. Witchcraft, on the other hand, has traditionally been taken rather more seriously, but also has the association with evil and devil worship. Witches were not seen as mere entertainers, but even when they were disbelieved there was still the idea they were up to no good. The combined associations of these two words in the modern consciousness means that today's pagans are variously viewed as wicked, deluded, and fraudulent.

The pagan conception of magic and witchcraft, however, is quite different. Magic essentially refers to the exploitation of phenomena not yet understood by science, while witchcraft is simply the term for a wide variety of folk traditions designed to produce "magical" effects. Here, we run up against what I consider to be a somewhat sneaky verbal sleight of hand by skeptics. The word these people love to use is "supernatural." They assert that the supernatural violates certain natural laws, and therefore cannot exist by definition. From this fairly sensible claim, they then make a logical leap to dismissing all apparently magical or miraculous phenomena as impossible. It happens so quickly and smoothly that most people don't notice it, but the second claim does not follow from the first, which makes it not only a logical fallacy, but an exercise in goalpost moving to boot.

What might be surprising to skeptics is that most pagans would not disagree with the claim denying the supernatural at all. Paganism is a nature-based religion, and is thus concerned with things which are natural. Indeed, everything in nature must be, by definition, natural. There is no need to result to the supernatural in order to explain the mysterious things we may encounter along the strange journey of life. But just because something is natural does not mean that we have a complete understanding of it, and it is perfectly possible that there exist many natural phenomena that remain unexplained or even unnoticed by the scientific community.

For example, a pagan might observe that witches and shamans have been effectively using placebos and hypnotism for medical purposes for thousands of years, to which the skeptic will retort that there is nothing supernatural about the placebo effect. Well, who ever said there was? Pagans do not claim that these mysterious effects are somehow outside of nature, merely that they work. Yet, when a scientific explanation is discovered for these ancient practices, skeptics act as if this somehow disproves the pagan worldview when in fact it confirms it. This is what I mean by goalpost moving. Skeptics elide from a claim that something doesn't exist to, when this is proved wrong, the obvious and uncontroversial claim that the phenomenon has a rational explanation. Of course it does; everything ultimately does. I repeat that magic refers to the exploitation of phenomena not yet understood by science, and makes no claims that they will never be understood. In any case, to return to our previous examples of placebos and hypnotism, if tricking the brain into healing the body absent any chemical medicine isn't magic, I don't know what is.

This leads to a point I want to make about uncertainty and the unknown. I would venture to say that pagans as a group are generally more comfortable with uncertainty than most people belonging to other religions. Recall that pagans have no holy books or sacred texts received from on high. There is no set of instructions, stamped with the divine seal of approval, telling us how we got here, what our purpose is, what rules we must follow, and what our reward will be for doing so. We have to figure these things out for ourselves, aided by tradition, community, and the sometimes half-baked theories of other mere mortals like ourselves.

A similar kind of uncertainty plays an important role in libertarian thought as well. The history of governments largely revolves around a single individual asserting competence to direct the activities of his subjects. As the size of communities expanded, tribal chiefs became kings, assuming responsibility for increasingly large numbers of people. It is perhaps unsurprising that these rulers began to assert a divine mandate to guide their actions. How else could they hope to convince the populace that one man could effectively govern thousands? One could even argue that the very concept of the divine right of kings reveals the fundamental weakness of their position. On some level, society has always recognized that the job of ruling is too big for one man to handle, hence the appeal to a superhuman intelligence to assist in the task.

Today, we've largely replaced the idea of kings guided by gods with presidents and prime ministers guided by advisers, generals, academics, experts, and that ubiquitous deity of the modern age science! I will have more to say about the problems with scientism a little later, but for now it is enough to point out that libertarians have always rejected the idea of central rule by one person, or even a large committee of people. The reason for this is the fundamental impossibility of possessing enough knowledge to effectively manage a complex society comprised of millions of individual actors.

It's easy to fall into the trap of regarding the citizens of a country as playing pieces to be positioned by our leaders in service of a larger societal goal. But not only do people each have their own preferences, goals, and aspirations, but they each have their own minds as well, often minds which are staggeringly imaginative and creative. I don't care how competent or smart you are, no one mind can hope to compete with the combined creative force of an entire society, nor should it try. When you leave people alone to figure things out for themselves, they're going to come up with solutions you would never have thought of in a million years.

When I discuss my vision for a free society with others, they often ask me very specific questions about how certain things would work absent central organization. How would a free-market supply health care, education, infrastructure, law enforcement, and national defense? As a common meme among libertarians goes, who will build the roads? These are perfectly understandable questions. We've grown used to seeing things done a certain way, and it's difficult to imagine how they could be otherwise accomplished. People desire security and the assurance that adopting a new system will not result in disaster, and who can blame them? Yet, the very nature of a free society means that these questions are difficult to answer. If I'm being truthful, I have to admit that for most of these questions, I genuinely don't know the answer. However, this lack of knowledge is not an admission of defeat, or a concession that I have not thought my position through. Quite the opposite. In fact, if I was actually able to answer these questions with any certainty, that would undermine my entire argument. The reason for this is that the point of allowing people to come up with their own solutions is that we don't know what those solutions are going to be beforehand. There is a discovery process, a system of trial and error, that is capable of producing surprising and wonderful results that a central planner would never have imagined. If, on the other hand, we did know exactly how, for example, education would be provided absent government schools, there would be no point in allowing the discovery process to work. We could simply impose the imagined solution from the top down and be done with it. It's the fact that we don't know that requires us to take a light hand in designing institutions.

This way of thinking is unsatisfying and even frightening to many. Certainty is comforting, and why take a risk on a change that may not work when we already have a system that, if not perfect, at least is not a complete disaster? Again, this is a good question, and in many circumstances, it is indeed prudent to refrain from action whose results are unknown. The difference here, as I see it, is that although we certainly don't know what the final result will look like, if you understand the nature of the process, you can be pretty sure that the result will be reasonably good, even if we can't predict the specifics of what it will look like. Remember that when people act, they are not doing so randomly. They are trying to achieve goals in the best way possible according to their particular circumstances. Thus, market solutions are not analogous to turning on a machine without understanding how it works or what it does. Because people can observe the effects of their actions and the actions of others, they can self-correct if things start to go wrong. They can switch strategies if their first attempts do not work. They can also communicate with each other in order to better collaborate and coordinate their actions.

When you impose a plan on society from the top down, however, you lose the benefit of all that communication, collaboration, coordination, and adaptability. People follow the plan, and if the plan turns out to be flawed or shortsighted, it will be carried through to its logical outcome regardless, even if that outcome is disastrous.

In summary, the market process isn't supernatural or foolproof any more than the magical techniques employed by pagans, but both involve an understanding that the universe contains a level of complexity inaccessible to the single mind, and the humility to allow that complexity to serve its function even if we don't quite understand what that is or how it works.

Subjectivism and Magic

The author Ayn Rand famously coined the term "Objectivism" for her philosophy of personal freedom, rational self-interest, and limited government. She claimed that her ideas were based on an allegiance to objective, demonstrable reality with no room for wishy-washy ideas about mysticism, divinity, or anything that could not be demonstrated through empirical observation. I think it's fair to say that part of her motivation for adopting this stance was her rejection of many of the doctrines of Christianity, such as an emphasis on altruism, self-sacrifice, and poverty. She saw these values as the ones which ultimately lead to collectivism and the type of communist state from which she escaped in her youth. Although the Soviet Union was explicitly atheist in its formation, she believed that religious teachings asking people to worsen their own situations in favor of others primed the citizens to accept a collectivist government and to feel guilty about asserting their own value as individuals.

Objectivism remains popular among libertarians, although Rand herself rejected both the libertarian label and its adherents (as she rejected pretty much everything that wasn't explicitly Objectivist.) Still, she remains a controversial figure even in libertarian circles, as many feel she went too far in proclaiming the virtue of selfishness, or at least communicated her ideas in such a way as to invite misunderstanding. Despite Rand's notoriety and association with libertarian philosophy, however, subjectivism plays a major role in the libertarian worldview, as it does in pagan beliefs as well.

Arguably the most important insight in the development of libertarian economic theory is the recognition that value – the amount of worth we place on any given object or service – is a subjective judgment made by each individual, rather than an inherent feature of those objects. For centuries, economists had struggled to explain why some things are expensive and others are cheap. A popular theory, accepted by Adam Smith as well as by Karl Marx, held that value was determined by the amount of human labor needed to create something. Others thought that value was related to the scarcity of an object, or how difficult it would be for the purchaser to acquire it through other means. None of these theories completely succeeded in explaining the prices observed in the real world, however.

In the 1870s, an Austrian economist named Carl Menger spearheaded what became known as the marginal revolution, with the insight that value is not an intrinsic property of objects at all, but simply a judgment made at a particular time and place, and that such judgments were made at the margin – meaning that a thirsty man might value his first glass of water more than his second or his tenth. This may seem obvious to us today, but at the time it was a revolutionary idea.

It's also an idea that even modern thinkers sometimes have a hard time putting into practice. People make the choices that seem best for them at the time, given their specific circumstances. Yet we still speak of people behaving irrationally or making wrong choices, as if there is an objective measuring stick by which to judge such things. Economist Ludwig von Mises countered this viewpoint by upholding the principle of subjective value, writing, "If a man drinks wine and not water I cannot say he is acting irrationally. At most I can say that in his place I would not do so."

This way of thinking is not merely a matter of economic interest it underlies the entire worldview of the libertarian. As outside observers, it is simply not possible for us to determine what the "right" or "wrong" choices are for any given individual; it all depends on their circumstances, their preferences, and their values, all of which are unique to them. And if we can't critique these choices as "wrong," then we are certainly in no position to impose the "right" choices upon others through the force of law. This is not to say that there should be no laws, or that everything is subjective. Libertarians believe in protecting life and property from thieves and murderers, for reasons both pragmatic and relating to a theory of natural rights too involved to cover here. But when it comes to telling other people what to eat, drink, smoke, wear, buy, sell, or trade, we generally think that it's better to mind our own business.

As I've grown older and become more experienced, my worldview has grown increasingly subjective, partly as a result of studying economics, religion, and linguistics. Language in particular provides an interesting example of example of subjectivism in action. Despite what certain dictionary and style guide editors will tell you, no one is "in charge" of language. It emerges organically through the complex interactions of countless individuals. Words are merely noises (or in the case of writing, shapes) that certain groups of people have arbitrarily decided have meaning. These meanings are not intrinsic to the sounds themselves, but the result of an operation that takes place in our brains. The precise nature of these operations change all the time, resulting in subtle shifts in semantics, spelling, and even grammar. Thus, language is constantly changing and evolving. No one language is better than any other, and as long as you are able to accurately communicate your meaning to other people, you cannot strictly be said to be using language wrongly. What conventions there are simply exist to facilitate comprehension, and to signal various levels of formality and education on the part of the writer/speaker. The oft-heard complaint "that's not a real word!" is fairly meaningless outside the confines of Scrabble. Dictionaries don't decide what counts as a word, as should be evident from the many neologisms that occur each year as a result of rapidly changing technology and culture.

This was not always clear to me. As a youth, I was a celebrated rule follower and stickler for procedure. Like many young minds struggling to make sense of a world that was comparatively unfamiliar, I desired to put everything into a readily comprehensible box, secured from disruption by a lid of ironclad logic. It took many years for me to recognize the limits of such an approach to life, and I've since come to regard it as rather a juvenile way of thinking. The real world is far too complex and full of exceptions to fit into any artificial constraints we attempt to impose.

A deeper understanding of language and economics was an important part of my intellectual development away from being a snotty little prescriptivist. Another revelation came from reading a book on vision. Having rather poor eyesight, I was trying to better understand how the eye works, and in doing so was amazed to discover that the way we experience the world is just as subjective as the price of bread, perhaps even more so.

We tend to think of objects as having certain characteristics that we can detect with our eyes. "That's red, blue, shiny, dull, bright, dark, etc." In reality these qualities, much like prices, are not objective properties of physical substances at all, but our subjective experience of them. What we experience as vision doesn't take place in the outside world, but inside our own heads. Our eyes take in information via light, and our brain interprets that information as pictures, but there's no reason that need be the case. We could just as easily interpret light as sound, as smell, as taste, as touch, or as something completely different. Nothing really is red, for example. We just experience redness as a way to differentiate different wavelengths of light.

So, if the pictures of the world we see when we look around don't actually exist except inside our heads, it's not a difficult leap to imagine that all sorts of other seemingly objective phenomena are merely illusory, or vice versa. This is where magic comes in.

There is considerable disagreement about what magic is, how it works, if it works, and whether the results it obtains (or appears to obtain) are objective or subjective. The twentieth century English occultist Aleister Crowley defined magic as "the art and science of causing change in accordance with will." Under this broad definition, magic encompasses everything from flashy paranormal phenomena to making a cup of tea, and science itself becomes a subset of magical techniques. A contemporary of Crowley's, Dion Fortune, was trained in psychology and adapted his definition into a more subjective one. She calls magic "the art and science of causing change in consciousness in accordance with will." In this formulation, it is not the world that is to be manipulated with magical techniques, but ourselves. As seen above in the vision example, the boundaries between these two things can sometimes be a bit fuzzy.

Does magic work? It depends on who you ask and which definition they use. Most pagans will generally say "yes," but the mechanism by which magic acts is considerably more controversial. Some regard magic as a way of tugging on invisible strings that connect seemingly unrelated phenomena to bring about results that seem, on the surface, acausal. To these people, magic is like science, the manipulation of energy to create effects, with the only difference being that we don't really understand how magic works yet. Once we do, it will no longer be magic, but be transferred over into the realm of science. There is nothing supernatural about magic, as all things that exist in the natural world must be, by definition, natural. There are simply aspects of nature than we still know very little about, and it is those aspects which the magician is interested in, not to explain them, but to use them as tools for the benefit of himself and others.

Magic is, therefore, an ever-shrinking category of effects which can be observed but which are not comprehended or recognized by the scientific establishment, and we can imagine a possible future where magic vanishes entirely as our knowledge of the natural world approaches completeness.

It is also possible to view the mechanism of magic as entirely subjective. In this characterization, magical techniques are basically psychological tricks designed to get the mind into a certain state. The elaborate use of props, including colors, sounds, incense, and other ritual tools, are designed to assist in altering consciousness to produce a desired result. The result comes not from some mysterious unseen benefactor or the manipulation of objective reality, but due to a change in how the operator interacts with the world. For example, suppose you want to cast a spell to attract money in a time of financial need. You would arrange all the appropriate items, invoke the appropriate gods and spirits, and intone the appropriate words until you are convinced that the spell has worked. At that point, it may appear that opportunities for enrichment suddenly fall into your lap, but a more likely explanation is that the confidence and determination gained from the mere act of being proactive have enabled you to more aggressively pursue avenues likely to result in financial gain. Someone who goes out job hunting every day is more likely to get rich than someone who sits on the couch watching television, and it's possible that the magical act is what was needed to inspire more productive action. In large part, this is what Aleister Crowley was talking about when he said "do what thou wilt." It's your task as an actualized human being to discover what you really want, what your purpose is if you prefer to phrase it that way, and then to do what it takes to go get it.

All this is not to minimize or deprecate the idea of magic. It can be tempting to read "it's all in your head" as dismissive, but it isn't meant to be at all. First of all, I'm not saying that it is all in your head, although I think that's very likely a part of it. But even if it is, that's no knock-on magic's power or efficacy. The mind is an incredible and incredibly mysterious organ. We know that it is capable of miraculous feats when pressed, from healing apparently terminal illness to granting enormous strength at need. If magic is able to tap into some of those mental powers at will, I can only see that as a remarkable credit to practicing pagans and magicians everywhere.

The larger point here is not to convince you to believe in magic – only those who have worked it successfully are likely to be convinced – but to point out that a healthy appreciation for subjectivism is central to both libertarian and pagan thought. Those who are unable to appreciate or see the value in individual, personal experience, or those who insist that their viewpoint is the only correct viewpoint, are unlikely to find much sympathy with either the pagan or libertarian way of thinking about life, nature, and society.

Stasis and Motion

One surprising viewpoint that seems to unite libertarians and pagans is a rejection of the idea that the universe, and the role we play in it, is a static or stationary thing. At this point, you may be asking yourself what in the world I am going on about. Everybody knows that the Earth moves around the sun and that the sun travels through the galaxy, and even the galaxy itself spins at breakneck speed as it hurtles through the universe. Surely, then, no one seriously entertains any ideas about a static universe, do they? Well, perhaps not in the abstract, but when it comes to how people actually behave and discuss life on a local level, it seems that stationary thinking is all too common and this way of thinking has implications for how we organize society.

For example, classical economics, the kind you are likely to learn in a college course on the subject, has long perpetuated the idea of economic equilibrium. When the needs and wants of buyers and sellers intersect, and the price for a particular good is agreed upon, the market is said to be in equilibrium. When, on the other hand, we observe shortages or surpluses, when prices seem too high or too low, and when the powers that be worry that consumers are not spending enough, classical economists consider this equilibrium disrupted. When this happens, it is common for policy makers to suggest that the government should take action to correct the problem and restore the market to its natural state of equilibrium. This can involve expanding the money supply, creating tax incentives, or even forbidding the use of certain prices as in rent control or minimum wage laws.

To the libertarian economist, the idea of a stationary equilibrium is a mere fiction. The market, understood through a libertarian lens, is not stationary in the slightest, but is in fact a continuous process through which individuals constantly adjust their actions to changing conditions. This adjustment may drive prices towards a hypothetical equilibrium, but to the extent that such a concept even exists, it is certainly not a place of rest. It is, rather, simply the direction towards which economic activity tends, and itself is constantly changing and shifting with external circumstances.

This explains the libertarian skepticism about central economic solutions to perceived market failures. If you throw a monkey wrench in the form of artificially low interest rates or bailouts for failing banks into a system that is in the process of self-correction, you are more likely to make things worse than better. It is preferable to stand back and allow the process to work unhindered, until it starts working properly again. This is somewhat analogous to the care doctors have to take to avoid interfering with an immune system fighting an infection. In most cases, letting antibodies do their job will result in a speedy recovery, although the healing process may be characterized by some unpleasant symptoms. Try to suppress those symptoms too aggressively, and you end up disrupting the process and making the long-term illness worse.

Libertarians are often criticized for having a blind, almost metaphysical faith in the market, and for attributing seemingly magical properties to it. In fact, we simply have some insight into the nature of complex systems made up of many millions of moving parts all working independently of one another. From a bird's eye view, these systems may resemble chaos, but in reality, all those independent actors are working towards a common goal, in this case a well-functioning economy. Libertarians believe that many minds working to solve a problem are more likely to stumble upon a solution than one central planner thinking he knows enough to right things on his own. The market, remember, is not a thing. It's just the name we give to the combined actions of millions of contributors. These actions are always in motion, and any attempts to make them settle down into a stationary equilibrium are sure to end in disaster.

The inherently mobile nature of all things is also a cornerstone of pagan thought. When most people look at a stone or a piece of wood lying on the ground, they imagine these objects as dead, lifeless, immobile. Pagans do not see the world in this way, however. The pagan world is one made up of energy, and energy is never at rest. One of the seven hermetic principles laid out in *The Kybalion*, a foundational occult text, is the Principle of Motion, stating that all objects vibrate, and that stillness is an illusion. Of course, modern inquiries into quantum mechanics have proved this to be literally true, but it's a notion that dates back thousands of years, to at least the ancient Greeks.

In the Qabalah, a system of Jewish mysticism that was heavily influential on ceremonial magic techniques and remains popular with some varieties of pagan, it is taught that the universe itself does not simply exist, but that it is continually being created. Energy from a divine source (whatever you imagine that source to be) is constantly pouring into the world, imbuing it with life, and should that energy ever cease to flow, we and all that we know would wink out of existence. In this conception, the universe too is a process, not something that is, but something that happens, every hour of every day.

Those who tend to view the world of matter as a static and dead thing are dismissive of the pagan relationship with the Earth, the stars, and the subtle energies whose manipulation we call magic. But viewing the universe as a living thing not only expands our methods for interacting with it, but increases our sense of reverence and awe at the world that surrounds us.

The Seen and the Unseen

That Which Is Seen and That Which Is Unseen is the title of a very important essay by the French laissez-faire economist Frederic Bastiat. Bastiat used the parable of a broken window to illustrate that most of what happens in an economy is invisible to the average observer, and that politicians and planners make the mistake of trying to address the most noticeable problems without considering what problems those solutions may create behind the scenes. In the essay, it is observed that a broken window provides work for the town glazier, and must therefore be good for the community. If no windows ever broke, all the glaziers would be out of a job, surely an undesirable outcome. But Bastiat points out that this is only part of the story. Yes, the glazier gets paid to replace the window, but what would have happened to the money had the window not broken in the first place? The answer is that it would have been spent on something else, providing employment elsewhere. Perhaps the window owner would have bought a new pair of shoes, employing the cobbler. Once the window breaks, the glazier may be happy, but the cobbler is out of luck. Nor is this a simple tradeoff between two competing interests. The glazier's gain is the cobbler's loss, but it is also a loss for the owner of the window. He could have had a window and a new pair of shoes, instead of using his money to replace something that need not have broken in the first place.

The insight that destruction is not beneficial may seem obvious, but you'd be surprised how many policies are built around this counterintuitive assumption. For example, it is commonly held that the Second World War was responsible for ending the Great Depression, as if sending soldiers and machinery overseas to be killed or destroyed could possibly be good for a country. Imagine what we could have done if we had kept all those men alive to engage in productive activity here at home, instead of losing their lives in an expensive conflict.

Note that I am here offering no judgments about the morality or necessity of the United States entering that war; it may well have been right and necessary to do so. But the economic argument that bombs and slaughter are good for business is simply nonsense, in the same way that you can't improve an economy by wantonly breaking windows.

Even smart people are not immune from the Broken Window Fallacy. Nobel laureate economist Paul Krugman has made the argument that anticipating a war with extraterrestrials, and preparing for that war by building weapons, would stimulate economic growth and provide employment for the masses, even if these imaginary adversaries don't exist and the war never comes. What he overlooks is the unseen effects of diverting resources from useful enterprises – food, housing, medicine, consumer goods – to useless ones – weapons for a war that never comes. Half a moment's thought makes it clear that it's better to do useful things than useless ones, but it just goes to show how easy it is to overlook Bastiat's "that which is unseen".

This is why libertarians favor a light touch when it comes to public policy. It's very easy to fixate on one element of the economy while ignoring others, and end up doing more harm than good. We must always pay strict attention to that which is unseen, or else risk making blunders that can cost lives or livelihoods. The policy maker who is suckered into the belief that war creates prosperity quickly becomes a menace to society if he is allowed to put his ideas into action.

The need to look beyond the obvious and search for unseen forces that can have an impact on our lives is one place where libertarianism and paganism are in sympathy with one another. Indeed, much of pagan belief is grounded in the idea of unseen worlds that exist in parallel with our more commonplace, physical reality. Magic, as defined by pagan practitioners, involves making contact with, and manipulating these hidden forces to bring about results here on the physical plane, as well as to gain knowledge about ourselves and the world we live in.

The practice of divination, integral to many varieties of paganism, is an example of this latter technique. Divination can be practiced in innumerable different ways, but the goal is always the same: to gain insight into a particular problem of living and to obtain guidance on how to proceed. Divination is distinct from fortune telling in that pagans don't claim any certainty over what will happen. In fact, there is no such answer. A great many things may happen depending on the choices we make and the choices of others. But divination can provide insight into the forces at play and the direction in which those forces tend at any particular time.

Thus, astrology is a form of divination, in which the unseen forces of stars and planets – their light and gravitational pulls – are observed with respect to how they affect the Earth and its inhabitants. Those who scoff at astrology usually have a highly simplified version of the practice in mind, in which everyone born on the same day must necessarily have the same temperament, and the position of celestial bodies determines the outcome of events. Of course, such claims are easily disproved, but the genuine pagan makes no such claims in the first place. The stars impel, they do not compel. The positions of stars, planets, and constellations, are but a few forces among many, and while they are believed to have an impact on world events, that impact is not so great as to overwhelm all other influences. In his small book *Synchronicity*, psychologist C.G. Jung conducted a study of married couples based on star signs and found a correlation of harmonious relationships to those signs which are supposedly compatible. This is just one study, and correlation does not prove causation, but Jung was open to the idea that astrology might indeed have some small influence on human behavior. I myself was formerly a skeptic of astrology, until I began to notice certain patterns in my own relationships, in which particular star signs cropped up a statistically improbable number of times. These are the kinds of "meaningful coincidence" which Jung refers to when he talks about synchronicity. Of course, one need not be a believer in astrology or in divination in general to live a pagan lifestyle, but pagans in general tend to be more open minded about the influence of unseen forces than those of a more materialistic mindset.

Other forms of divination include the reading of tea leaves, the casting of runes, observing signs and omens in the plant and animal world, introspective meditation or trance, and, most commonly, the use of tarot cards. Tarot itself is an extremely deep and fascinating subject about which many volumes have been written. Far from a mere fortune teller's tool, the 78-card deck tells an esoteric story of the Fool's journey from which much occult wisdom can be derived. There is a great deal of (mostly apocryphal) lore surrounding the origin of the tarot deck, but the cards in their modern form appear to have originated in seventeenth century Italy as the ancestor of our modern playing cards. The main difference between tarot decks and the cards we use to play bridge or poker is that tarot decks, in addition to the four numbered suits, contain 22 "Trumps" or "Major Arcana" cards depicting people and concepts such as The Magician, The Hermit, Strength, Justice, and Death. When used in a divinatory context, the meanings of these cards are not as straightforward as the names would indicate, and require the interpretation of a skilled diviner taking into account context, as well as the numerous correspondences that have accrued to each card over years of development. In addition to its name and image, each card is linked to a planet, a zodiac sign, an element, a time of the year, a number, a Hebrew letter, and a path on the Qabalistic Tree of Life, as esoteric diagram purporting to explain the nature of existence and the order of creation.

A proper study of the tarot takes a lifetime to undertake, although a rudimentary reading can still be of use to a novice just purchasing their first pack of cards. But there is essentially no limit to how deep you can go into the cards if you so choose. What do a set of cards shuffled at random have to do with anything meaningful, you may ask? Like all forms of divination, the cards are merely a conduit through which we connect to the hidden energies operating behind the scenes. A properly attuned reading can access these forces to influence both how they deal the cards and how they interpret them, and in this art is the true divinatory power of the tarot. In theory, a sufficiently advanced mystic could achieve the same result without the need for the prop, but the cards with their evocative illustrations and communal significance built up over centuries of use serve as an invaluable aid to getting oneself into the right frame of mind for a spiritual experience. Much of what pagans call magic could be called (somewhat cynically) a form of self-hypnosis; the extent to which these experiences are objective as opposed to subjective is a matter of belief that differs from person to person.

Anti-Utopianism

One of the major criticisms libertarians have with other forms of political ideology is the tendency towards Utopian thinking. There is a belief among many people that it's possible to design a perfect system that corrects for all injustice, poverty, and cruelty in life if only we think hard enough about the problem. To this end, these people elevate those whom they perceive as extremely intelligent to positions of great power, trusting that a carefully selected panel of scientists, philosophers, university professors, and engineers will be able to use their skills to "fix" society and create something akin to paradise on earth.

In America, progressivism emerged in the early twentieth century based around the ideas being explored in the scientific community. Charles Darwin's work on natural selection and the evolutionary process, as well as Gregor Mendel's demonstration that pea pods could be selectively bred to alter various characteristics proved particularly influential to the nascent progressive movement. The United States elected Woodrow Wilson, a college professor, as president, trusting in his superior brainpower to lead the nation onward and upward towards an ever brighter tomorrow. Wilson, like many of the progressives of his day, saw what Darwin and Mendel had done, and wondered whether the same principles might be brought to bear on the human race as well. If pea pods could be made taller, stronger, and better through selective breeding, why not people as well? Thus, the science of eugenics was born.

It's seldom remembered now, but eugenics was fairly enthusiastically embraced in the United States before the Nazis gave it a bad name. Tens of thousands of American citizens were forcibly sterilized, often without their knowledge, all in the name of improving the race. Bad genes were to be filtered out and good ones encouraged; what could be more logical than that? As philosopher Karl Popper pointed out in *The Open Society and Its Enemies*, the danger of Utopian social engineering is that a complete redesign of society from the top down requires a master plan, and in order for that master plan to work, anything that doesn't conform to it must be stamped out. This is why you so often see horrific human rights abuses from those who claim that they just want to make everything better.

The important point about the above story is that, from a purely scientific standpoint based on the evidence available at the time, the eugenicists were behaving rationally. Had their program been allowed to continue, it might even have worked. But by divorcing scientific theories from morality, empathy, religion, compassion, and all the things in life which can't be measured and quantified, they found themselves committing atrocities without even realizing it. The central failing of scientism is the misapplication of natural science techniques to human institutions, treating people as if they were no more than cogs in a giant machine. You can always depend on a cog to fulfil its function without a fuss, and you don't have to worry about hurting the cog or its feelings. But humans are not like cogs. Our behavior is not predictable because, unlike cogs, we have the ability to choose. And unlike a cog, you can't just disrupt a person's whole existence because you are not happy with what he is doing and how he is doing it.

Pagans and libertarians both view human beings as something more than mere automata to be moved around at the whims of others. There is something special about our wills, our ability to choose and plan, and our capacity for suffering. Whether you derive this outlook on humanity from something like a divine spark or from some other source, it follows that people have certain rights that ought to be respected, and that the pursuit of individual happiness is something meaningful to be preserved, not merely to be bent towards some collective higher purpose without our consent. If every man and woman is a star, then it seems profane to manipulate them without the due respect or awe for their majesty.

Insofar as politics is concerned with individual rights, then, it seems logical that those of us who reject the scientistic conception of society would search for a set of policies consistent with a more holistic, if not necessarily metaphysical, view of the human condition. Libertarians, being politically minded sometimes to a fault, have settled on a few such policies which I would imagine many pagans would be sympathetic to.

The flip side of a tendency towards Utopianism is an unfortunate tendency to see every problem as a fatal flaw indicative of the need for systemic change. If Utopia is the goal, and a Utopian system is possible, then any observable suffering must be evidence that the current system is bad and needs to be replaced with something better. This is what often lies behind violent revolutions. Frustrated citizens would prefer to burn everything down and start from scratch, rather than trying to bring about gradual and incremental change within the existing framework of society. It probably need not be added that these revolutions have seldom worked out for the good during the course of world history, and that Utopia remains elusive.

Libertarians don't believe in Utopia. They recognize that people are flawed and that therefore their institutions are always going to be flawed as well. Perfection does not exist on Earth, or anywhere else as far as we know, so the best we can hope to do is improve things on a piecemeal basis, one change at a time. And they believe that the best way to do this is basically to leave everybody alone and let them pursue happiness in their own way, as long as it doesn't hurt other people.

Utopian thinking is not unique to politics; it exists in religion as well. The promise of eternal paradise is a key feature in many of the world's most popular faiths, and it's easy to see why. What better carrot to attract followers than the idea that not only is death not the end, but that what comes after will be totally free from pain, sadness, grief, and want? Of course, here again the belief in a potential paradise is not without its pitfalls. Holy wars, terrorist attacks, and mass suicides have all been partially motivated by a desire to more swiftly attain that promised perfection. The incentive problem is obvious: if you tell people that death is infinitely better than life, odds are you're going to see a lot more death than would otherwise be the case.

Paganism makes no such promises about paradise, nor does it imagine that perfection is attainable here on Earth. We can strive to improve our spiritual position and understanding, but the struggle is a continuous one. In fact, paganism as a whole doesn't have much to say about life after death, at least not with any real unanimity. You will certainly encounter pagans who believe in reincarnation and who will be happy to tell you about their many interesting past lives, and that is certainly one valid way of thinking about the spirit's journey after physical death. But the truth is, we don't really know, and I've not met anyone who seeks to impose a particular theory of the afterlife on anyone else.

Not necessarily having a great beyond to look forward to, I like to think that pagans are more appreciative of the here and now, of living in the moment (which is, after all, one of the chief goals of mindfulness meditation). And like libertarians, they are able to appreciate the progress we've made without the frustration of continually failing to live up to an impossibly high standard of perfection.

Two Kinds of Materialism

Speaking of appreciating what we have, there's another way in which paganism differs from other religions, and that is in its attitude towards the very world we live in. Christianity has the doctrine of Original Sin, that mankind is fallen and requires redeeming. Buddhism teaches that life is suffering, and that escaping the material plane entirely is the only solution. The notion that the world as we experience it is somehow corrupted and wicked is shared by Judaism, Hinduism, and Islam as well. The end goal of all of these faiths seems to be the same: to get out. All in all, it's a pretty gloomy attitude to carry with you your whole life.

Paganism has no such doctrine about the degraded or fallen nature of the material world. Physical reality is regarded as only one of a number of overlapping realities, but by no means an inherently bad one. In fact, other worlds such as the astral plane, are just as likely to be home to dangerous or malevolent entities as our own environs, maybe more so due to their unfamiliarity. There are good experiences and bad experiences to be had wherever you go, and while extensive travel can certainly be beneficial in expanding your outlook and understanding, there is nothing wrong with wanting to come home again after a long and weary sojourn.

I've elsewhere described paganism as a nature-based religion, and that should give you some clue as to the attitude pagans hold towards the material world. Yes, the Earth contains much that is painful and cruel, but there is also plenty of beauty, kindness, and love out there if you look for it. Flowers, trees, waterfalls, rainbows, and sunsets are a part of that, and the stereotype of the modern pagan as a bit of a hippie is not without a certain foundation, but there's more to it than that. Nature doesn't just mean plants, rocks, and animals. It means the world as a whole, and that includes us humans. There is a tendency to think of people as being somehow outside of nature, with everything we do being unnatural by definition. But humans are just as much a part of nature as deer and rabbits. We arrived by the same process. We are not opposed to nature; we are an integral aspect of it. I'm not entirely sure where the idea that nature and mankind are enemies came from, but I suspect it has something to do with the attitude expressed in the Bible that God created man to have dominion over all the plants and animals. This is unfortunate, because both as pagans and as libertarians, we have little interest in dominion, preferring to see ourselves as part of a larger whole that is mostly out of our control.

This attitude towards humanity's place in the world casts human activity in a rather different light. If we regard it as natural for beavers to build dams and for bees to make honey, why then should it be any less natural for people to build skyscrapers or make Flamin' Hot Cheetos? One could argue that all these species, including humans, are simply acting according to their nature, and that there's nothing wrong with that. This is not to say that we have license to drive species to extinction or bulldoze natural wonders on a whim; as part of the world we have a responsibility to treat it with respect and a certain amount of reverence. We should be as reluctant to tear down a thousand-year-old oak as we would be to destroy the monoliths erected by ancient people. But it does mean that we need not view all that humans do as inherently wicked and all that animals do as inherently good, for we are animals too.

Because pagans don't hate their lives and the world, as Jesus advises his followers to do (John 12:25), they are likely to treat their environment with a bit more care, while taking time to rejoice in the wealth of beauty available to us, from manmade things like music and architecture, to the forests, seas, and mountains that remain largely untouched by human hands.

The pagan appreciation for the material world must not be confused with materialism. While today this word is typically used to mean an obsession with money and consumer goods, in philosophy it denotes the theory that the universe is composed of matter and only matter. To the materialists, there is no world other than the one we can experience with our senses, albeit amplified at times by scientific instruments. Thoughts, dreams, emotions, and spiritual experiences are written off as the byproducts of chemicals interacting within the bags of meat we call our bodies. Many materialists even deny the existence of free will, arguing that our decisions are dictated by a purely material interaction between the chemicals in our brains and our environment. Choice, they claim, is an illusion.

The implication of this view is that, if we had perfect knowledge of the state of the universe at its creation and of the laws of physics, we would be able to deduce what the president of France is going to have for breakfast tomorrow, as well as every other human decision that ever has or will be made. This is not the place to go into an in-depth discussion of the question of free will, one which has plagued smarter men than me for hundreds of years, but suffice it to say that pagans don't really buy into this deterministic view. As mentioned before, paganism carries a belief in multiple planes of existence which include (depending on who you ask) the material, etheric, astral, mental, and spiritual planes. And while divination with tarot cards, runes, astrology, and a number of other methods is a common pagan practice, diviners do not see this as contradicting the idea of free will. "The stars impel, they do not compel" is a frequently heard aphorism, meaning that while divination can be useful for discovering likely or potential future events, it does not make fixed or unbreakable prophesies. Indeed, one of the best reasons for using divination in the first place is to discover possible future pitfalls so that they can be avoided, something which would be impossible if we lacked the free choice to alter our actions accordingly.

Chapter 6

Liberty as Personal Philosophy

To this point, I have dealt primarily with libertarianism as a political philosophy and with paganism as it relates to theology, and some would argue that it would be best to leave things there. Strictly speaking, they may have a point. There are good arguments to be made that neither system is or should be a holistic philosophy encompassing all of life, but rather quite narrow answers to specific questions. Libertarianism deals with the proper application of political force, and has little to say about anything else. Paganism seeks to answer a spiritual question, leaving more material issues to other disciplines. Still, I can't help but notice that there are certain personality traits and attitudes that tend to go along with these philosophies. That is to say, it is pretty common to turn the lens with which we view the world inward, and convert a political or religious idea into a more personal philosophy about how to live, what to value, and what to oppose. In this chapter, I want to take a closer look at what makes individuals who are attracted to either pagan or libertarian ideas tick, and to see whether those basic drives overlap in any significant way. In other words, let's see whether pagans and libertarians may be temperamentally compatible in addition to sharing certain views about how the exterior world works. It will not surprise the reader at this point to learn that I believe the answer to be a resounding yes.

Nonconformity

In my last book, *Conform or Be Cast Out: The (Literal) Demonization of Nonconformists*, I was interested in the ways that society has developed a hatred and fear of those who are different throughout history, often going so far as to identify dissenting individuals with evil or the Devil himself. Many of the victims of this practice turned out to be pagans, whose willingness to practice a minority religion made them a target for dominant power structures looking for scapegoats. The reason this issue spoke to me so vividly was that I've always been attracted to people who think differently, and have even suffered my own fair share of attacks from those who found my ideas dangerous or threatening.

In order to be a nonconformist, you have to be able to think for yourself. It is easy to go along with what your peers, your family, your church, or your government tell you is right. It takes both courage and brains to reject these deeply held ideas in favor of something new, and courageous, brainy people are, if not always admirable, at least interesting.

Pagans are great nonconformists. They dress funny, engage in seasonal rituals that most people would consider weird at best, profess a belief in things others scoff at, call themselves witches and routinely employ symbolism that mainstream society has associated with unspeakable wickedness for centuries. In order to be willing to live like this, you've got to have at least a little bit of a perverse streak in you that delights in, or at least doesn't mind, the dangers of being different. Some pagans flaunt their nonconformity while others try to hide it, but even the shy ones are sufficiently contrary to be willing to buck a huge number of societal norms in order to act out their beliefs. Good for them.

Libertarians are similarly contrarian by nature. It takes guts to advocate for radical change to institutions most believe are absolutely sacrosanct. Doing so incurs a price, albeit not one nearly so severe as what early pagans had to endure at the hands of their oppressors. Throughout my time in politics, I've been accused of being greedy, selfish, heartless, ignorant, stupid, and even evil for daring to dream of a free society. People get angry when you challenge their core assumptions about the world, but being an iconoclast is all in a day's work for the champions of liberty. We don't like to be told what to think, even by people who otherwise agree with us. This tendency can sometimes work to our own detriment, and is largely responsible for the constant factioning we see in libertarian circles. We get hung up on arguing with each other about the morality of driver's licenses and other minutia while losing sight of our larger shared goals. That's just one of the occupational hazards of holding a "don't tell me what to do" mindset.

When some pagan friends and I decided to read a book about the spiritualist movement in America for our monthly book club, I was struck by the amusing similarities between these intrepid mediums and women's rights activists and some libertarians I know today. They don't get much mainstream coverage, but the spiritualists were an impassioned force for gender equality in medicine, among other fields, using the public fascination with occult phenomena as a gateway into broader civil rights issues. Overall, a highly interesting and inspiring group of women, and politically not dissimilar from the proto-libertarians operating at the same time. But they suffered from so strong a resistance to central control that any attempts to organize on a large scale broke down, as members stormed off in a huff declaring "no group can contain me." Personally, I find this attitude relatable, admirable, and not a little charming, but I'm also reminded of the difficulties modern libertarians have in getting organized without being consumed by internal squabbles. I've also been reliably informed that this is a problem faced by many pagan organizations, tending to fracture whenever leadership is perceived as too controlling or dogmatic. Again, good for them.

As difficult as it can be dealing with contrary and independent personalities, however, there are lots of plus sides as well. A personal tendency towards nonconformity spills over into every aspect of life, meaning that if you're willing to risk running in these admittedly weird circles, you're certain to encounter a lot of interesting and unusual hobbies, interests, and activities. My libertarian friends are musicians, standup comics, civil war reenactors, medievalists, anime enthusiasts, and artists. My pagan friends are herbalists, candle makers, astrologers, dream interpreters, pole dancers, mapmakers, and librarians. I know brewers in both movements. They invariably have good taste in literature, movies, and music. I myself have a passion for strange industrial and noise records, and have variously dabbled hobbies ranging from juggling and fencing to the study of dead or nearly dead languages. Conformity may be boring, but pagans and libertarians never are.

Attitudes Toward Power

Power is a word with a wide variety of meanings, some more sinister than others. Power can mean the ability to dominate and control others, but it can also refer to self-actualization and the ability to control the circumstances of your own life. Someone with a great deal of power can be a tyrant, or can be free from the shackles of tyranny. Lord Acton observed that power tends to corrupt and absolute power corrupts absolutely, and this is a maxim that libertarians have taken deeply to heart. Skepticism about concentrated power is at the heart of the libertarian ethos; we know that those with the ability to control us will eventually be tempted to do so in selfish or irresponsible ways, and so we seek to prevent anyone from acquiring such power in the first place. The flip side of this is that we also want to empower individuals as much as possible in order that they might resist any efforts to control or coerce them. Power, being a fact of life, should be dispersed rather than concentrated, thereby minimizing the damage any one individual or faction can do.

There is a stereotype about libertarians that they hate the government but worship corporations, and much friction between libertarians and those on the political left comes from this misunderstanding. The left fears the power of big corporations just as the right fears the power of big government, and both are correct in their anxieties. However, what both sides too often fail to understand is that these two power structures feed off one another. They are not antagonistic forces pulling in opposite directions; they are collaborators who share both goals and the means to achieve those goals.

I've always considered corporate power as fundamentally distinct from government power in that corporations are not allowed to use violence to compel their workers or customers. No matter how rich a corporation may be, they cannot force me to buy their product or work in their factories. They may make tempting and convenient offers, but if I say no, I'm not going to jail or getting shot. This all changes, however, when corporations send their lobbyists to Congress in order to ask for special favors. Under the guise of consumer protection or a sense of fair play, these lobbyists will convince legislators that their competitors are misbehaving and need to be restricted in some way. Frequently these restrictions come in the form of regulations that look to the untrained eye like the government rightfully holding corporate excesses in check. A high corporate tax rate, mandated employee benefits, complex and costly record-keeping requirements, environmental protections, licensing or accreditation requirements all have every appearance of being an annoyance to big companies and a boon to consumers. It may, then, seem inexplicable why the world's largest companies spend millions lobbying in favor of such regulations instead of against them. The reason for this is actually quite simple. Far from being motivated by a public-spirited sense of guilt and compassion, the world's richest corporations know that they can afford these regulations better than their actual or potential competitors. With their deep pockets and army of lawyers and tax accountants, it's a small matter for them to negotiate miles of red tape in order to pursue their business. On the other hand, if you or I attempted to start a competing company, we would quickly find ourselves drowned in bureaucracy and impossible to meet expenses. Thus, the authority of the dominant firms goes unchallenged.

Ever wonder why there's only one cable provider in your neighborhood and you have to put up with their high prices and terrible services whether you like it or not? It's because other companies are legally not allowed to enter the market and compete with them. It's one of many examples where government and big business team up against the consumer. Corporations can't directly compel you to buy their products, but they can leverage the legal system of government to get their way all the same, and that's the real danger. Progressives are right to be worried about corporate power, but they fall into the trap of thinking the solution is to give government more regulatory authority, when we have seen time and time again that this authority is simply captured and employed in the service of the richest and most powerful. Libertarians are no fans of corporate power, despite what the stereotype says. What we want is dispersed power, minimal coercion, and a citizenry strong enough to stand up for itself.

How do we achieve that? By opposing efforts to rob the citizens of their greatest tools for resistance: the freedom of speech to criticize bad ideas and promote good ones, and the right to bear arms as a last resort against tyranny. This is also why a strong economy is so important to libertarians, because a wealthy population is better positioned to resist authority than one that is poor and starving. The love of money may be the root of all evil, but a comfortable income allows you to live the life you want to, not the one forced on you by others.

Personal empowerment and independence is important to pagans as well. Indeed, the practice of mindfulness, meditation, and magical techniques are all designed to increase the individual's ability to control his or her own life without having to submit either to the desires of others or to the contradictory impulses of our own minds and bodies. As anyone who has struggled with temptation knows, sometimes we can be our own worst enemies when it comes to living a happy, healthy, and productive life. Meditation and a focus on developing the powers of the will, all important aspects of esoteric training, help you conquer your passions and take a more conscious role in directing your activity.

The idea of personal empowerment also plays into how pagans relate to and interact with gods, spirits, and other non-physical entities. We've grown used to the idea of a god as a cosmic figure of authority. In the monotheistic religions, god issues commands and instructions about how to live, and threatens punishment for failing to obey. In the Old Testament in particular, god routinely engages in displays of power in order to encourage submission and obedience. Humans defy god's will at their peril. We see this in stories from the Garden of Eden to the Tower of Babel. But even in older religions, gods tended to be pretty demanding. The Greek and Roman myths are filled with stories of unlucky mortals who end up on the wrong end of a divine personality. The gods punish hubris or idolatry, but also randomly take sides in purely human conflicts, as in *The Iliad*, where being on the wrong side in a war could be enough to incur some pretty cruel treatment from Ares or Athena. Sometimes all you had to do was unwittingly end up the victim of Zeus' seductive powers to find yourself tortured or killed by his jealous wife. In fact, it seems the best strategy for surviving in Ancient Greece was to simply keep your head down and hope to escape divine attention. There's a reason the term "god fearing" has enjoyed such popularity over the years.

Modern pagans have a rather different attitude toward their gods. While we acknowledge the power of spiritual figures and take pains to avoid deliberately insulting them or abusing their favor, neither do we regard them with trembling fear. Instead, we regard them as potential partners, with whom it is possible to build a fruitful and mutually beneficial relationship. Through reference and the occasional offering, both spiritual as well as physical, pagans believe that they can coax divine figures into helping out with the problems of everyday life. One may invoke various gods in spells for things like wealth, love, courage, strength, good luck, and forbearance. A ritual invoking Pan may be used to reduce timidity and bring out the inner wild child, or Thoth for assistance in acquiring knowledge and wisdom. It is not uncommon for pagans to leave out saucers of milk or beer to encourage the protection of household gods and fairies, to aid in a more harmonious domestic living situation.

These activities, useful though they may turn out to be, are optional, however. You are not obligated to make regular sacrifices or even to name any deities in your practice. Some pagans don't believe in these gods at all, and neglect them without apparent difficulties. Thus, the gods of modern paganism are not authority figures to be feared and obeyed, but potential collaborators to be approached, or not, as you see fit. Of course, if you do choose to pursue a relationship with a deity, it is important to recognize that doing so is not without danger, but that danger is easily avoided with the proper precautions, and need not be entered into at all if the thought of such things makes you uneasy.

In this sense, gods are extensions of our personal power, enabling us to accomplish things we might otherwise be unable to do. The belief in their existence expands our sphere of control over our own circumstances. It doesn't restrict it by imposing sacred duties or prohibitions on us. A world inhabited by gods makes us freer, not less, and that way of thinking is entirely consistent with the libertarian ethos.

License and Responsibility

A common criticism I see leveled at libertarianism is that it's a licentious philosophy, an anything goes free for all with none of the rules or accountability necessary to bring order to society.

"We can't let everyone just do whatever they want, it'll be chaos" they howl, imagining a hedonistic society devoured by sex, drugs, and rock and roll. There are doubtless a few libertarians who think this actually sounds pretty good, but it's not a fair or accurate representation of what the philosophy is all about. Libertarianism is not about eliminating responsibilities; it's about devolving those responsibilities down to the level of the individual. It's obvious that some amount of rules, structure, and discipline is necessary for society to function. That's not in dispute. What is in dispute is where those rules ought to come from in order to maximize happiness, well-being, and personal freedom.

Pagans fall prey to the same attacks from members of religions with a more rigid system of authority. If god is dead, then everything is permitted, goes the famous aphorism, but conversely if everything is permitted, what effect does that have on god? Fortunately, we need not answer these weighty questions, for everything is certainly not permitted, not under any ethical system I have experienced anyway. What pagans and libertarians have in common on this point is a feeling that a sense of responsibility and duty is best found within the self, and that to outsource that feeling to a separate authority is a bit of a copout. If all the information you need to know about how to behave can be found in a set of divine commandments, then you need do no reflection or thinking for yourself. You're off the hook, just do what the book says and, ethically speaking, you're in the clear. Likewise, if the state legally prescribes which behaviors are acceptable and which are not, that takes the burden of any soul searching off the back of the individual citizens. If something is illegal, one need not question whether it's right or wrong. Just obey the law and everything will be fine. Conversely, the same thought process can lead one to conclude that everything which is legal must be ethically fine. If it were a problem, the state would prohibit it, right? And if they haven't prohibited something which turns out to be wrong, well they have no one to blame but themselves. They should have been more vigilant.

It's obvious that this line of thinking is seriously flawed, and will result in either a society of children ever looking to their parental figures for guidance, or of automata, incapable of deviating from the program that has been written for them. What pagans and libertarians want is a society of responsible adults who have to determine for themselves how to behave in various situations. There will be mistakes, to be sure, but those mistakes will land hard on the conscience of the transgressors, forcing them to reflect and reconsider how best to act in the future. Under such a system, the outsourcing of responsibility, and therefore the abdication of guilt, and therefore the loss of an opportunity for growth, is simply not possible.

Robin Wood makes this point elegantly in her ethics workbook for pagans:

> We don't have to follow small laws, and codes. Our Gods don't stand over us, saying 'Don't steal.' We don't have rules, because we don't need them. We understand why stealing is wrong; we avoid it because we love others and seek never to harm them. Because we know that they are just as real, and just as important as we are. We don't need to be threatened with a hell full of fire and brimstone to keep us from injuring one another.[9]

In the pagan community, as in the libertarian one, individuals are expected to develop a sense of interior ethics, and to be held personally responsible for their actions. A rigid set of prescriptive rules not only isn't needed in such a system, it actively undermines the ethos of accountability to the self and to the community.

I can tell you're skeptical, so let me give you an example. A couple of years ago, I learned about an experimental system of criminal justice being employed in Longmont, Colorado. The practice is known as restorative justice, and instead of focusing on punishment, it is concerned with making the victim whole to the greatest extent possible. If an item is stolen, it has to be restored. If property is damaged, it must be repaired. If something irreplaceable has been lost, the victim and the offender must work together to find a way to make amends in a mutually agreeable way. Most revolutionary of all, is that restorative justice removed the court and prison system from the equation entirely, placing the restoration process in the hands of the community. Both victim and offender have to consent to the process in order for it to go forward, so no one is being forced into anything against their will.

When people first hear about restorative justice, their response is usually to scoff, dismissing it as some hippie-dippy, touchy-feely, soft on crime approach that would never work in the real world. But it does work, and Longmont has the statistics to prove it. Before the program was implemented, the police talked about how they would see the same faces over and again, as repeat offenders gradually settled into a lifelong cycle of crime and punishment. Today, the recidivism rate for those who go through the program is virtually zero. How is this possible? Because of the power of personal responsibility.

Under the traditional justice system, things are cold and impersonal. Offenders are dragged before a judge, then forced to serve a sentence or pay a fine, and then released. Rarely do they even face the people they have wronged. Under such circumstances, it's easy for a petty criminal to feel unfairly treated and to become resentful. Once inside a penitentiary, the offender is surrounded by other criminals, eager to confirm their biases and teach them further methods of criminality. Even those who mean well can often find themselves forced back into unlawful activity by the stigma of a conviction or a period of prolonged separation from productive society. It's no surprise that most prisoners find themselves on the wrong side of the law again shortly after being released.

The restorative justice process, on the other hand, forces offenders to look the people they have wronged in the eye, to see the hurt that they have caused, and to accept that their actions are responsible for another person's suffering. It's hard to overestimate the effect that can have on a person. A young vandal or shoplifter raging against the machine can be completely transformed when he sees the small business owner struggling to feed his family due to missing inventory or the costs of property repairs. The responsibility for the crime falls on his shoulders alone, and cannot be shrugged off as a failure of church or state, and that makes all the difference.

Longmont's restorative justice program is a practical example of the kinds of personal responsibility that both libertarians and pagans would like to see flourish in broader society. It's easy to be cynical and sneer that there will always be people who have no conscience, and who will try to cheat the system under any circumstances. It's undoubtedly true that such people exist, but they are certainly no less likely to try to cheat when they can abdicate all sense of responsibility onto someone else's shoulders than when they have to face up to it themselves. The decline in Longmont's recidivism rate tells us that maybe these hypothetical sociopaths are actually fewer than we like to imagine.

It's also important to point out that an endorsement of personal choice does not equate to an automatic endorsement of those choices. There's an assumption that because libertarians oppose drug criminalization, for example, that we all want to be high all the time. Not so. There are libertarians who use drugs enthusiastically, but there are just as many who abstain entirely. I've never personally used an illicit drug in my life, nor do I have any desire to do so. But neither do I believe that my personal choices give me the right to prescribe those same choices for others. The same goes for any other sort of behavior that does not directly harm other people. I may disapprove of it, even publicly condemn it, but there's a big difference between that and using the threat of force to control other people's actions. Many people struggle to grasp this distinction, and accuse me of endorsing any behavior, however ghoulish, that I do not believe should be legally prohibited. That people can't even conceive of leaving choices in the hands of individuals just demonstrates how far away from an ethic of personal responsibility we've drifted.

Chaos Magic and Freedom from Habit

Self-help books and lifestyle gurus frequently talk about the need to break bad habits and replace them with good habits. When the urge for alcohol rears its ugly head, why not drink a glass of water instead? Instead of settling in for an hour of television every night, take that hour and spend it jogging. Use the body's natural tendency towards inertia to your advantage, by ingraining behavior that will make you healthier, wealthier, and happier.

This may be good advice as far as it goes, but the goals of libertarianism and paganism are not health, nor wealth, nor even happiness. To many, they revolve around personal actualization, independence, and self-determination. In short, the discovery and fulfillment of the magical will.

From this perspective, good habits are only slightly less harmful than bad ones. Habit itself can be viewed as a danger preventing the individual from reaching his full potential. After all, freedom doesn't refer only to liberation from external oppressors, but from internal ones as well. It is just as possible for a man to be a slave to his own impulses as to those of a king or tyrant, as anyone with experience with addiction will know.

Much of the aim of magical practice, particularly meditation exercises, is to gain conscious control of otherwise unconscious processes. This is what Renaissance magicians referred to as contact with one's holy guardian angel, and probably what Crowley meant when he talked about discovering the True Will.

When we start to meditate, the first thing we notice is how little control, or even conscious knowledge we have over our body and mind. Assuming a meditative posture for the first time, we are amazed at the body's unwillingness to obey. Aches, pains, itches, twitches, and spasms of all kinds spontaneously emerge in rebellion against the act of remaining stationary for a prolonged period. Attempting to bring our breathing under control prompts a similar revelation, namely that the breath wants to do its own thing and rebels against the slowness and regularity demanded of it. The mind is the worst culprit of all, for the second we attempt to silence it, we become aware of all sorts of chaotic thoughts whirling just beneath the surface of our consciousness, thoughts that refuse to go away, and twist like a captured animal under any attempts to subdue them.

When I first began to practice meditation in earnest, I was stunned at the lengths to which my mind would go to try to escape stillness and reflection. The minute I closed my eyes, thoughts would spring up unbidden designed to disturb my practice.

"You need to pay that bill!"

"You haven't practiced the guitar in a while. You should do that now!"

"Shouldn't you make a cup of tea before you start this?"

"Isn't it time to go check the mail?"

The efforts of my subconscious to get me to do absolutely anything except meditate were so transparent that I often found myself laughing out loud at them. Each time, I would simply say to myself "that can wait, we're meditating right now." Eventually, these distractions grew fainter and sometimes, though not always, they disappeared altogether. When this happens, I know I have succeeded in bringing my mind and body under conscious control of my will.

Habit, whether good or bad, is another subconscious process that must be brought under control if the individual is to obtain true freedom. The goal is to freely choose every action you undertake, not simply obey the urges brought about by instinct and habit. Indeed, it is this ability to choose that separates humans from lower animals. We have the ability to overcome our biological programming and exercise the will to achieve our goals, whatever they may be.

In other words, when you study for an exam, it should be because you choose to, not because you are in the habit of studying. When you commute to work, you should choose your route so as to arrive on time, not simply blindly follow the same set of turns you do every other day. Likewise, when you engage in so-called "bad habits" it should be because you are making an affirmative choice, not because you are obeying an addiction or following the path of least resistance. It is only when we choose our actions that we are truly free, and at our most human.

To achieve this, Crowley, in his book on meditation, recommends that we set about acquiring and breaking habits almost at random until the force of habit loosens its grip. At first, it is best to pick something with no moral connotations in either direction to avoid clouding the issue. For example, maybe you can spend a week tugging your left earlobe every time you say the word "hello", just to see if you can do it. Or, you could try to spend a day without saying the word "is" or without putting your hands in your pockets. These simple, self-imposed mandates or prohibitions force us to be mindful of our behavior, to act rather than react, and over time they will help the will triumph over habit as the chief driver of action.

The literature of chaos magic, a school of occultism focused on pragmatism and iconoclastic disregard for tradition, frequently advises an even more drastic application of the above principle. In other words, habit should be abandoned to such an extent that our political views, religious faiths, moral sensibilities, and even entire personalities, should be subject to drastic change at will. The radical chaos magician views even the constraints of personality as a limit on personal freedom, and seeks to cast them off by adopting and discarding worldviews as if they were sets of clothing. After all, how can a libertarian be truly "free" if he can't also be a communist or a totalitarian? How can a prude be free if he is unable to embrace promiscuity and exhibitionism, and vice versa?

As a rhetorical point, this view holds some interest, but I would not advise anyone to attempt to follow it in practice. While the annihilation of the individual personality is indeed the goal of some systems of eastern mysticism, as a western individualist, I can't help but see more downsides than benefits to such an approach.

Chapter 7

Diversity, Tolerance, and Pluralism

Every Man and Every Woman Is a Star

In Chapter 2, we talked about a line from Aleister Crowley's *Book of the Law* which states "do what thou wilt shall be the whole of the law," meaning that it is up to every individual to discover and pursue their True Will or purpose in the world. Another line from the same book claims that "every man and every woman is a star." To me, this is a beautiful metaphor that sums up my attitude towards the primacy and dignity of the individual. You are important as a person, you matter. Don't hide your light under a bushel. At times you may appear like a small point of light floating in a vast, dark expanse of sky, but you have it in your power to nurture whole worlds, and the effort you put forth can be observed across vast differences of space and time. When you look up at the night sky, the light from the stars has travelled for thousands of years to reach your eyes. There's nothing small or insignificant about that.

Libertarians dislike collectivist thinking because it diminishes the importance of the individual in favor of some group, whether it be a nation, a political party, a race, a gender, or an abstract idea. To the collectivist, you matter only insofar as you work for the benefit of a larger organism. People who want to walk their own path or abstain from engaging with the collective are seen as vestigial at best and as an active threat at worst. In extreme examples, this can result in horrific human rights abuses, like those we saw under the Soviet Union where the good of the Party was seen as more important than the good of the individual, or under the Third Reich, where the glory and purity of the German Nation and the Aryan Race was prioritized above all else.

Libertarians believe that there is no higher good than individual self-determination. People are valuable for their own sake, not merely as they contribute to someone else's master plan. Thus, even when collectivist thinking doesn't result in death camps overt or oppression, it still seems pretty rude and disrespectful. Human beings are fascinating kaleidoscopes with a fantastic array of varied interests, abilities, personality quirks, and thoughts waiting to be shared with the world. Collectivism seeks to squash all of these unique traits under a single umbrella classification that, to the libertarian, crushes all the wonderful idiosyncrasies that combine to make you who you are. This is why libertarians reject identity politics and intersectionality. You are more than your skin color, your genitalia, your sexual preferences, your nationality, your religion, or your political affiliation. You're a person, and every man and woman is a star.

Individualism lies at the core of libertarian philosophy, perhaps more than any other single idea. Every person has value and dignity for their own sake, and therefore ought to be protected. This is the root of the concept of individual rights. You have the right to live your life and pursue happiness as you see fit, provided you extend the same courtesy to others. When we talk about rights, we tend to lapse into creating long lists of things that ought not to be infringed: the right to life, to own property, to speak freely, to religious freedom, to bear arms, and so on. In reality, all of these rights really stem from one simple claim: that you own yourself and your body, and therefore can do what you like with it. Others are not allowed to kill or attack you because that violates your right of self-ownership. You have the right to free speech, because attempts to forcibly shut you up infringe on your bodily autonomy. You have the right to own property that you either created or traded with someone voluntarily for, because you did those things with your mind and your body, which you own. The libertarian view is that as long as we protect the rights of individuals, the groups that they form will be protected by extension.

This notion renders the concept of group rights (women's rights, men's rights, victim's rights, minority rights, etc.) redundant. All of these are really just human rights, to which we are all entitled as members of the human race. Membership in a particular group should neither confer new rights or eliminate already established ones. It is certainly important to protect minority groups from the tyranny of the majority, but it is well worth remembering that the smallest minority of all is the individual. From this it is clear that things like racism and bigotry are products not of individualism or capitalism as some would have it, but of collectivist thinking. You can only discriminate against someone based on their group identity if you recognize group identities in the first place. The libertarian author Ayn Rand observed that 'racism is the lowest, most crudely primitive form of collectivism." If we judge people as individuals, it is impossible to be bigoted.

Individualism is probably not the first thing that comes to mind when you think of paganism. As we will see in the next section, groups and communities are extremely important to most forms of pagan practice. Yet, it has also been my experience that pagans see themselves as far more than mere members of a collective identity. The ones with whom I associate are intensely diverse in their interests, beliefs, and outlooks on the world. They also treat one another with respect and understanding, delighting in each other's differences rather than demanding conformity to a single set of norms.

In Robin Wood's workbook on pagan ethics, she explains why respect for the individual is so important:

Allow your friends their privacy. Allow them their own lives. Never force them to do something because you think it would be 'good for them.' Never, never assume that something would be good for someone else because it would be good for you. There are billions of people on this planet and every single one of them may travel hundreds of paths in their lifetime. Dear friend, please understand that the odds of meeting anyone in exactly the same spot on exactly the same path as you are vanishingly small. Each person is an individual case and must be treated as such. Please, please remember this.[10]

Libertarian economist and philosopher Murray Rothbard once wrote that it is respect for the value of individuals that makes freedom desirable in the first place. If men were like ants, he mused, undifferentiated and interchangeable, there would be no reason to care about their liberty at all. It is our differences, our different preferences, talents, attitudes, and desires that make individual liberty an end worth pursuing. I see this same respect and celebration of individuals in paganism as well. Every man and woman is a star, and while those stars may come together to form constellations, this does not diminish the importance of the individual. The whole is impossible without the part, after all.

While there are certainly groups within the pagan community that enforce a certain set of beliefs or values, I would argue that the religion as a whole is less dogmatic than almost any other, allowing adherents to express their individual attitudes towards faith in almost any way they wish. In short, the right to pursue individual happiness is recognized and celebrated, which seems to me a pretty libertarian approach to religious practice.

Inclusion

Pagans and libertarians are alike in that they embrace minority viewpoints often misunderstood and misrepresented by the mainstream. Perhaps because of this, as well as due to the nature of the philosophies themselves, both groups have a history of being less judgmental and more inclusive than their more popular counterparts. When Barack Obama and Hillary Clinton continued to voice their opposition to gay marriage, an opposition that remains in full force within the Republican Party, libertarians were already on the record saying that it's none of the government's business to dictate the kinds of relationships consenting adults can enter into. And while prominent Democrats have done a good job of disguising just how recent their conversion towards gay rights has been, they have consistently lagged behind libertarians in support for alternative lifestyles.

This is because the libertarian worldview doesn't view individual preferences or identities, whether they be based in race, gender, sexual orientation, or anything else, as the proper domain of public policy. Your life is personal to you, and no one else should have a say in how you live it, especially when it comes to the most intimate and private aspects of your experience.

Similarly, religion has long been regarded as the enemy of the LGBTQ community due to the prohibitions on homosexuality spelled out in the Bible and the Koran, prohibitions which unfortunately continue to be championed by people who are happy to leave the other Old Testament laws in the past where they belong. Paganism has no holy text demanding that we all follow a certain dogma, and is therefore more flexible to adapt with the times. More than this, though, paganism has always been more sympathetic to the non-traditional lifestyle. This is not surprising given that so many early practitioners were women living on the outskirts of mainstream society. In paganism's exaltation of female as well as male deities, and in the use of hermaphroditic figures like the Baphomet, it's clear that a complex interplay between the sexes has always been baked into pagan practice, and this has carried over and evolved as modern paganism has moved into the twenty-first century.

An article from the Washington Post recently declared paganism to be "the most LGBTQ-affirming faith in the US."[11] The article cites several specifically LGBTQ-focused groups within the pagan community and interviews faith leaders about their experiences within the community. While acknowledging that no space is totally free from prejudice and ignorance, these influential pagans argue that their religion affords them more acceptance than the rest of mainstream society in general.

This is a credit to paganism's decentralized nature, where different groups can focus on different issues that are important to their members without having to all subscribe to precisely the same ritual structure. So, while some Wiccans retain the traditional god-goddess polarity model, others have adapted it into something that is more palatable to those with non-binary gender identities. Just as there is room for a wide spectrum of opinions on how best to operate inclusively within libertarianism, that same diversity can be found in paganism, with enough different groups so that everyone can practice the faith the way they want to without being forced into a situation in which they don't feel comfortable or included.

Of course, intolerance can still be found in all sectors of society, and some groups preaching ethnic superiority, particularly in Northern Europe, have given some varieties of paganism a bad name. This is a pity, because such hateful views are certainly not representative of the broader movement, just as the few libertarians with ethno-nationalist leanings don't represent the fundamentally peaceful and tolerant political philosophy.

Hierarchy versus Community

While it is true that libertarianism is, in many ways, profoundly individualistic, this has led to some very common and deeply held misunderstandings about the libertarian attitude towards community in general. Part of this confusion is linguistic. Economic systems like socialism and communism have claimed a virtual monopoly over the words we use describing what it means to work together for a common goal. Socialism must be social. Communism must be focused on community. Therefore, anyone opposed to these ideas must be antisocial and anti-community. It's easy to see how this could lead people to come up with the wrong ideas.

Part of the blame is our own. Libertarians are notoriously bad communicators, and we have not done enough to discourage the stereotype of the ornery mountain man screaming "get off my land" while brandishing a shotgun. Henry David Thoreau made a great show of asserting his independence by moving out to the middle of nowhere and living by himself (although his actual social interaction was far greater than the text of *Walden* would lead you to believe.) Many of his contemporary nineteenth century classical liberals took a similar attitude towards society, deeming it oppressive to their individuality. In popular culture, to the degree we are depicted at all, it is as grumpy misanthropes like Ron Swanson from *Parks and Recreation*, a disgruntled and reluctant government employee whose attitude towards the general public is often one of open hostility. And this is the best-case scenario. Don't get me wrong. I love Ron Swanson, and find him both funny and likeable, but he does not exactly do wonders to help the libertarian brand.

While you will certainly encounter libertarians who appear to conform to the stereotype, by and large the philosophy is far more community focused than its detractors give it credit for. The reason for this is simple: we need other people to survive and thrive. Nor is this need begrudging or resentful. In many ways, other people are what make life worth living at all. Love, family, and friendship are all fundamental building blocks to a happy life, to say nothing of the economic conveniences of cooperation and collaboration. In his highly influential book, *The State*, German political theorist Franz Oppenheimer explained that there are basically two ways to get what you want. You can either take it by force, or you can trade for it, convincing people to voluntarily help you by agreeing to help them in return. Traditionally, dictators and tyrants have little need for cooperation or community. They can use the police, the military, and the courts to impose their wills on the public whether or not anyone likes them or agrees with their goals. In a democracy, this problem is somewhat lessened, but only somewhat. A strong enough majority can still force the minority to comply without having to resort to the sticky and subtle business of persuasion.

Libertarians reject the idea that other people get to tell you how to live your life just because they outnumber you. Your basic rights don't change based on whether they are popular or unpopular at any given place or time. That means that the only way we can interact with other people and influence their behavior is on a voluntary basis. If I want a farmer to give me food, I can't ethically point a gun at him and demand it. I have to persuade him to share his harvest with me. I can do this either by trading him something of value in return or by appealing to his sense of charity. One of these approaches is significantly more likely to yield results than the other, but both are possible, and both depend on a strong sense of community in order to function. In a world where voluntary transactions are the only way to get by, it is vital that we be able to form communities in which people look out for each other. If the hypothetical farmer above doesn't like me, no amount of begging is going to convince him to part with his food. If he doesn't trust me, it's going to be significantly harder to convince him to trade, even if the deal I offer seems good. You simply can't afford to be antisocial in a voluntary economy.

Paradoxically, government welfare programs designed to safeguard the vulnerable against selfishness and a lack of charity actually discourage this kind of pro-social mindset. If you are depending on other people to help you if you get into trouble, it is a good idea to be pleasant and honest in your dealings. It's also a good idea to cultivate strong friendships, family relationships, and ties to religious or other community organizations. The rugged individualist who neglects family, friends, and church does so at his peril, for who will be there to bail him out if he gets himself into trouble down the road? On the other hand, in a world where government assistance is readily available to everyone who needs it, these incentives largely disappear. You can afford to tell off your parents, move away from home into a strange city, make few close friends, and abstain from attending any community functions, safe in the knowledge that you need not depend on the goodwill of any of these people if you should fall on hard times. They will be forced, through their taxes, to pay for your upkeep whether or not they like or trust you. The allegedly pro-social policy makes it safe to behave in an antisocial manner, in a way that voluntary interactions do not.

In his last published book, *The Fatal Conceit*, economist F.A. Hayek explored the instinct for collectivist government policy among so many people, tracing it back to the way we function in very small, close-knit groups. In a tribe or a family, property is generally held in common. The breadwinners, whether hunters or factory workers, share their gains equally among their fellows, from each according to his ability, to each according to his need. Indeed, these institutions often work in much the same way that communists imagine that all of society could work, and this observation explains why the idea is so appealing. But Hayek pointed out that there is a crucial difference which makes such an arrangement unworkable as the size of a society grows.

In a family or tribe, accountability is maintained by the fact that everyone knows everyone else on a personal level, and can keep track of their activities. This means that shirking, cheating, and other dishonorable behavior that seeks to take advantage of the system for personal gain is quickly discovered and punished. Children know that if they don't do their chores and listen to their parents, they are unlikely to have a very pleasant childhood. A worker in a tribe who, like Bartleby the Scrivener, would prefer not to contribute, will quickly find himself expelled from the society, or worse. This is because deterrence of bad behavior is necessary for the survival of the group. If everyone suddenly decides to stop hunting, the whole tribe falls apart in a matter of days.

This system of accountability only works in very small groups though. Once a society exceeds the point at which it's possible to know everyone and keep them honest, it becomes easy to take advantage of communal property by taking more and contributing less than you really ought to, or are able to. And once it's discovered that cheating is possible, it's reasonable to expect almost everyone to start doing it, causing the near-instantaneous collapse of the whole society. In a voluntary economy, however, in which no one is coerced and people receive not some predetermined fraction of the whole, but what they can persuade others to give them through trade and charity, it is no longer possible to take advantage of the system in this way. You have to contribute something if you want something back, and you have a much better shot at receiving charity if you build a network of trusted individuals who know that you are not simply trying to dupe them with phony or exaggerated claims of hardship. Thus, contrary to the stereotype, a libertarian world would not be one of dog-eat-dog ruthlessness, but one in which we all depend on each other and behave accordingly.

In paganism, community is also important. Though this idea is perhaps not so often misunderstood as in libertarian circles, there are still certain misconceptions and stereotypes to be dealt with. We cannot escape the fact that for centuries, witches and pagans were regarded as outsiders, refusing to conform to the norms of their society and often isolated as a result. The image of the old woman who lives on the edge of town or the strange man who dwells in the woods as representative pagans is pervasive, though in most cases this derives from the attempt to escape persecution rather than a genuine preference for solitude. Recall that paganism stems from ancient practices from the early history of mankind, when isolation meant death and cooperation was the only way to keep the harsh realities of the world at bay. For this reason, group ritual and celebration has always been a fundamental part of pagan life. Whether it involves gathering together to mark the changing of the seasons and pray for a good harvest, or forming close knit groups (or covens) to engage in specific spiritual work away from the prying eyes of hostile busybodies, it was historically rare for pagans to practice their faith alone. This need for community was compounded by the fact that many practices were, until very recently, a solely oral tradition passed down through initiation ceremonies only to those who were deemed trustworthy to hold the sacred knowledge. Before the twentieth century and the dawn of the information age, anyone who wanted to learn about paganism as it was actually practiced (as distinct from secondhand accounts in history books) had a difficult time on their hands unless they happened onto others who could tell them about it, as Gerald Gardner claimed to in his meetings with the New Forest Coven. Trust, as well as mere numbers, was necessary in order to preserve the traditions and ceremonies of old. When Scott Cunningham published his very popular book *Wicca: A Guide for the Solitary Practitioner*, it was a revelation for many, as well as a heresy for some. Before that time, solitary practice was difficult at best, and some pagan leaders maintained that practicing the faith outside of the structure of an organization was simply not done. You had to be initiated by a priest or priestess to truly belong to the faith; anything else was just playacting. What's more, publishing Wiccan secrets in a book available to anyone and everyone seemed like a betrayal of the secrecy that had been a feature of various pagan groups since going against the Christian orthodoxy became dangerous, thousands of years before. Fortunately, these attitudes are far less common today, and many people pursue pagan ideas on their own without a problem. Still, community is highly valued and can be beneficial even for someone who chooses to do most of their spiritual work in the safety of their own home.

There is another practical reason for pagans to favor groups, and that is the increase in energy available when a crowd gathers for a united purpose. A lot of what pagans attempt to accomplish in their rites and rituals involves the raising and directing of energy towards a particular goal, and it's no surprise that the energy of two can be more effective than the energy of one. You've felt this if you've ever been at a packed concert with hundreds of people sharing a simultaneous experience of joy and excitement. You can feel the energy of the crowd crackling through the air. In many rituals, the goal is to create this kind of atmosphere among participants and then direct that energy towards doing something good, whether it be trying to influence a particular outcome or simply showing gratitude and devotion to the divine. The most striking example of this is the May Pole dance, held on May 1st, called Beltane by pagans. Dancers take hold of the ends of ribbons attached to a central pole, and then duck over and under one another, creating a beautiful woven pattern. As the music gets faster, the energy of the dancers increases until it reaches a frenzy, and ordinary consciousness gives way to something more sublime. Similar effects can also be achieved through group meditation, and the use of sound, colors, breathing, and movement. Of course, wearing yourself out with high energy dancing, chanting, or singing also creates certain vulnerabilities among the participants, so a certain element of trust is crucial to maintaining a healthy and safe ritual environment. I wouldn't necessarily want to engage in all of these activities with perfect strangers, which is why community matters so much to pagan practice.

Speaking of energy, it's also worth noting that part of the pagan worldview involves subtle energetic connections between all life forms. In Hinduism, they teach that all is Brahman and that any appearance of separateness is really an illusion. While paganism is not as doctrinally monist as Hinduism, a similar outlook of interconnectedness is pretty common. The bonds of community are strengthened by the notion that we are all part of a greater whole, and that even the trees and animals around us play a part in that structure. At first, this may sound like it directly contradicts the fundamentally individualist tenets of libertarianism, but I don't think it does. Just because I am invisibly connected to my neighbors doesn't mean that I can abuse them, steal from them, or dictate to them how to live. I have to respect their separateness while at the same time acknowledging our unity. Hurting others seems doubly foolish and evil when you realize that, in the process, you're also hurting yourself.

Humility

If I had to ascribe one cardinal virtue to libertarianism, it would be that of humility. The central motivation for a free society is to let everyone pursue their own version of happiness in their own way, because no one person, no king, no president, no scientist or economist, can know what is right for them under their own particular circumstances. Life is a complex thing, and try though we might, we can never really put ourselves into another person's shoes and fully understand their struggles, their hopes, their dreams, and their fears. It's up to each person to choose a path and walk it, to discover their True Will and enact it. No one else can do it for you, and in that sense it's a responsibility as well as a liberty.

Libertarians are skeptical of sweeping, top-down solutions to problems not only out of respect for individuals, but because we understand the dangers of unintended consequences. No matter how good your plan looks on paper, there's never any guarantee that something unforeseen, something terrible may happen once you put it into practice. And the bigger the plan, the more damage it can cause if it should happen to go awry. When you let people manage their own lives, a single mistake can indeed have catastrophic effects; one life, or even the lives of an entire family can be ruined by someone who lives foolishly and irresponsibly. It is natural to want to intervene to prevent this suffering before it happens. But we forget how much worse the suffering can be when these same foolish, irresponsible people are given the power to affect not just their own or their family's lives, but the lives of millions of strangers as well.

In China, Chairman Mao Zedong had a grand vision to modernize his country, gaining access to the industrialization that had enriched the West, and raising the standard of living for all Chinese citizens. He thought he was smart enough to bring about these changes – changes which had taken many decades to unfold elsewhere in the world – singlehandedly over the course of a few years. He called his plan The Great Leap Forward, but unfortunately, he forgot to look before he leapt. Mao assumed godlike authority in his country, not only relocating farmers to the cities in order to ramp up manufacturing, but diverting rivers and other natural phenomena to suit his designs. To stop birds from consuming the country's crops, he enlisted children to kill them on sight with stones. Everywhere Mao saw a problem, he assumed he had the solution, and he wasn't shy about using force to impose them.

The story of Maoist China is rarely talked about in the West today, even though it happened less than a century ago and resulted in more deaths than Nazi Germany and the Soviet Union combined. The farmers didn't know how to work the factory equipment, and there was no one to grow food while they attempted to learn. The rivers, diverted away from their rocky beds, disappeared into sand and soil. With the bird population decimated, insects swarmed unchecked and devoured what few crops remained. The result was the worst mass famine in recorded history, with an estimated 70 million Chinese citizens dying in the process.

Mao's sin, like the sins of so many would be rulers, was hubris. He believed that he could organize society better than what had been produced by thousands of years of voluntary cooperation among the people. He lacked the humility to see that there might be more to the structure of a society than what his limited mind could perceive. And he is not alone. History is littered with little Mao wannabes, as well as with the bodies of their victims. Vladimir Lenin, Pol Pot, Hugo Chavez, Fidel Castro, and yes, Adolf Hitler, all thought that their plans would work, and in every case the result was ruination and death.

It is easy to dismiss these dictators as psychopathic madmen, motivated by hatred and killing for fun, but in every case, it was good intentions that paved the road to Hell. All of these men had idealistic visions of shining Utopias without hunger or want, where everyone worked together for a common goal. Nor were these men simply too stupid to carry out their ambitions. Most of them were highly educated individuals of extreme intelligence, and that in itself contributed to their downfalls. They were too smart to see how foolish they really were, and trusted to their own brains when they should have looked around at the countless others managing their own affairs just fine without help from any narcissistic autocrat.

Writer and political philosopher G.K. Chesterton introduced the thought experiment known as "Chesterton's Fence". He explained that if you come across a seemingly pointless fence in the middle of an empty field, you should take the trouble to investigate why the fence was built in the first place before deciding to tear it down. Maybe the fence really is pointless and removing it would cause no harm, but maybe it is there for a very good reason. It is prudent to find out which of these is the case before acting, lest you inadvertently invite disaster. People like Mao ignore the lesson of Chesterton's Fence, casually sweeping away whole institutions that had stood for thousands of years without bothering to investigate why they had proved so durable in the first place, and the result is invariably catastrophic. They lack the humility to imagine that someone else might know something they don't.

There is good reason for pagans to sympathize with this respect for ancient, seemingly archaic traditions. After all, the entire pagan worldview could easily fall into that category. To the modern, enlightened, atheist types the folk rituals, seasonal celebrations, communication with gods and spirits, and the belief in an unseen world appear to be nothing more than tired superstitions with no practical value to today's busy lifestyle. But they too neglect Chesterton's Fence, in failing to even ask what purpose these traditions may have originally served, and may continue to serve.

Indeed, paganism is a humble faith in general. Pagans humble themselves before the power of nature, before the power of the gods, before the majesty of the universe in general. Unlike the Abrahamic religions, pagans do not imagine that the world was created specifically for our purposes, that we were "made in the image of god", or that we have been given dominion over the beasts and plants of the world. We are merely one part of creation, and while the human life force does contain analogs to the structure of the universe (as above, so below) that does not give us the right to dominate others or impose our wills on them.

Paganism also contains the humility that comes from mystery and imperfect knowledge. We know that the physical plane that we experience on a day-to-day basis is but a fraction of the worlds that exist. We know little enough about our own environment, to say nothing of the astral, etheric, and divine planes that exist outside our ordinary perception. We can perhaps get glimpses of these planes through meditation and trance, but the amount we actually know, either through direct experience or the teachings of others, is dwarfed by that which remains mysterious. It takes humility to admit the true limits of our understanding and allow for possibilities that may not have occurred to us – or to anyone else – before.

Finally, pagans practice humility through their lack of dogmas. This is related to the previous point. Since we understand so little about how magic works, we do not presume to tell others when they are doing it "wrong". Indeed, the proliferation of many distinct pagan practices all over the world proves that there is no one correct way to practice the faith. What works for Pacific islanders may be very different than what works for Nordic people, a Haitian priestess, or an Italian witch. The assumption that they may know something we don't is baked into the modern understanding of paganism, and it would therefore be wrong, not to mention rude, to go around like missionaries "correcting" what other people have been doing for many generations. In paganism, everyone is free to walk their own path, and while some may be faster or more effective than others, it is not our place to judge unless specifically asked for advice.

Complexity and Pluralism

We live in a complex world, and like most complex things, it can be difficult to understand even under the best of circumstances. Many people are uncomfortable with this. They would like to imagine that there are easy solutions to life's problems. If we can find the right formula, the right set of instructions, then all we have to do is follow them to get good results. This is appealing because it doesn't require a lot of critical thought, which is hard, and it doesn't leave us saying "I don't know" too often, which can feel like an admission of weakness or failure. This is why we see people chasing one fad diet after another in a continuous, but ultimately unsuccessful effort to lose weight and keep it off. The real path towards a healthy lifestyle is not as simple as "cut out carbs" or "go vegetarian"; if it were, new health gurus wouldn't continue to pop up every couple of years peddling new theories about nutrition. Yet the appeal of such reductionism is such that programs with demonstrably poor success rates continue to attract new followers every day. It's easier to buy into a flawed system, then make excuses when it doesn't work, than to grapple with the far more difficult task of accepting and embracing the complexity of the human body, not to mention life in general.

Compared to other religions, paganism is liable to seem to an outsider like a bit of a mess. It has no central, authoritative text telling followers what to do, how to behave, or even what to believe. The ritual structure is looser and more individual than those found in more prescriptive religions. If you become a pagan, no one is going to tell you that you have to pray five times a day facing Mecca, that you must abstain from pork, that you must confess your sins on a regular basis, or that you must forsake worldly possessions in favor of some higher spiritual truth. Of course, you can do any of those things if you feel so moved, but unless you voluntarily enter into an organization with strict rules, there is no authority figure demanding obedience to a particular set of dogmas. Whether you find truth and light in meditation, in building a shrine in your home to the Morrigan, or in performing elaborate rituals involving robes, candles, and incense, no one is likely to tell you that you're "doing it wrong" or "not a real pagan." Even such traditionally cherished practices as having priests and priestesses fill specific roles in rituals have been challenged and adapted in recent years by those who find this binary gender formulation limiting. In short, pagans are encouraged to find whatever works for them and pursue it however they like so long as in doing so they are not hurting others.

Libertarians are similarly eclectic. Again, there is no central text to which we must all swear allegiance. Although many libertarians are admittedly obsessed with certain books and authors which they will encourage you to read, do not be fooled into thinking this is a membership requirement. I've met plenty of people who have never read any of the books I would consider to be classics of libertarian thought, yet who still have an instinctive understanding of the basic principles of liberty. I would regard these people as the political equivalent of the many practitioners of traditional forms of magic and witchcraft around the world who have been happily practicing their faith without the need for formal initiations or Gerald Gardner's conception of what witchcraft consists of.

The reason for these parallel attitudes is, I believe, quite similar. It involves the understanding and embracing of the notion that the world is very complex, and that no one person or group is likely to have all the answers. We don't try to tell you how to do things, because at the end of the day we don't know what is best for you or what will work best in your particular circumstances.

The embrace of complexity also explains why libertarians are skeptical of centralized solutions to complex problems. It is easy to fall into the trap of imagining that we can wave a magic wand, pass a law, impose a regulation, or elect a politician who will suddenly make everything all better. In practice, this almost never works out. The reason is that society is made up of many different individuals, all with different interests, desires, preferences, passions, and needs, and each of whom has free will to change their behavior in response to changing conditions.

This is also one of the reasons that libertarianism tends to be cosmopolitan and pluralistic. We recognize that it takes all sorts of people to make a world. As long as people are cooperating peacefully and minding their own business, we don't much care what they do, where they come from, or what they look like. We are equally puzzled by nationalist types who judge people based on which side of an imaginary line they were born on, and by those who engage in identity politics, implying that your skin color, gender, or sexual orientation matters more than the way you conduct yourself and treat others.

It should be noted that there does exist in some libertarian circles an unfortunate strain of puritanism, gatekeepers who will try to shame you for not being as much of a libertarian as they think you ought to be, for not holding the "correct" policy positions, for not reading the right books, or for not subscribing to the theories of a particular author. Take no notice of such people. They are simply trying to build up their own sense of intellectual superiority by putting other people down, despite the fact that such actions are highly counterproductive to the hard task of building a movement and putting together coalitions. There is no Pope of libertarianism, and no one gets to tell you which views you're allowed to have. The good news is that we as a community have begun to recognize that this is a problem and are taking steps to discourage purity tests and the like. It is certainly possible that you may have a had a bad experience in speaking with a libertarian in the past, but I would encourage you not to let that color your opinion of all of us. Like many ideologies that fall somewhat outside the mainstream, libertarianism seems to attract some degree of social awkwardness and poor communication skills, but I assure you that we are not a monolith, and most of us would be happy to engage you in a friendly dialogue without judgment or derision.

Non-Evangelism

For most people outside of a particular faith, evangelism tends to be one of the least attractive qualities of religion. It is not enough for everyone to believe and worship as they please; some feel the need to impose those same beliefs onto others, without much considering whether their audience might enjoy being preached at. The same can be said for political philosophy, with zealots of all varieties demanding that you agree with their perspective on the world, and determined to keep haranguing at you until you either acquiesce or close the door in their face.

Sometimes the motivation for this kind of browbeating is understandable; Christians don't want their friends and loved ones to go to Hell, so obviously they view it as an act of love to try to save the otherwise damned. Political activists believe that they are on the right side of history, and in a democratic system where every vote counts, quiet disagreement is an obstacle towards achieving or protecting the kinds of human rights they regard as most important, or most under assault. Other times, the motivations for evangelism are less honorable, involving the collection of money or swelling of numbers for whatever "the cause" happens to be. Whatever the reasons, it's equally understandable that innocent bystanders don't like being told what to think, and would generally prefer just to be left alone.

Paganism is, attractively, a non-proselytizing religion, mostly uninterested in increasing the number of practitioners through self-righteous sermons or the distribution of informational pamphlets on street corners. Part of this is due to the secrecy which has necessarily characterized much of pagan practice for the last thousand years. Covens were formed within close-knit communities and subsisted on trust. When the penalty of publicity was persecution and death, one could hardly afford to go around indiscriminately recruiting. More generally, though, paganism's lack of evangelism has to do with its parallel lack of a claim to absolute truth. Pagans have no sacred texts, no dogmas, and no belief in eternal punishment for noncompliance. They don't think that everyone else is wrong if they don't subscribe to exactly the same views on ritual, deity, and magic. There are many paths to the top of the mountain. Why, then, should you demand that anyone switch their path to your own when you will both ultimately reach the same destination, particularly when your path is getting crowded as it is?

I suspect there's also a certain pride in many, though certainly not all, pagans in the feeling of exclusivity that comes from practicing a minority religion with an initiatory component. There can be a sense of achievement from membership in a restricted community, especially if the only way to attain such membership is through some non-trivial rite or ordeal that most others cannot or will not undergo. Too much evangelism can dilute this exclusivity and rob the community of its specialness, at least in the minds of some participants.

In the sphere of political philosophy, you will certainly find plenty of libertarians not immune from the pleasures of proselytizing, especially when they have succumbed to the dubious activity of trying to attain elected office. Yet, I increasingly believe that evangelism is inherently inimical to libertarian values. Free thought, as well as free speech, is a core tenet of the philosophy, and by that logic there cannot be much good in trying to change people's minds when they do not wish their minds to be so changed. One might even see forceful demands for unity of thought as a kind of aggression. I confess that we are now venturing further into my own personal philosophy than to libertarian orthodoxy, to the extent that there is such a thing, but one consequence of my deeply-rooted belief in human freedom is that the tactics of the salesman, who wants to sell you something you have no interest in, have become at best distasteful and unpleasant to me. I call this position intellectual pacifism, in which we do not make unwanted intrusions into the thoughts of others, just as we make no such intrusions into their homes. A man's ideas are his own business. If he is curious and eager to seek out new ones (such as those contained within this book), I will be happy to provide them. If, on the other hand, he is content with his current views and has no desire to change them, what right have I or anyone else to try to make him do so?

Just as with pagans, I suspect that many libertarians enjoy the same sense of exclusivity, and by extension superiority, in the holding of unpopular and altogether radical opinions, and really who can blame them? It's sometimes fun to swim against the current. After all, if everyone believed the same things, what a dull world that would be.

Chapter 8

Balance and the Tree of Life

As I write this, the world is in a somewhat tumultuous state. Political polarization is as bad as I have ever seen it, extremism is on the rise, and personal relationships are breaking down under partisan demands for loyalty and obedience. Under these circumstances, it's natural to wonder what's going on and whether there's anything we can do about it. Religious leaders of all faiths assert that our society is experiencing a spiritual drought, that atheism and materialism have deprived life of its beauty and purpose, and that the result is widespread depression, anxiety, violence, and nihilism.

It seems likely that there is at least some truth in this, although it's also no doubt an oversimplification. Those periods of history in which the church was dominant – and the modern countries governed by theocracy – are hardly free from problems. It is clear that faith alone will not cure society's ills, and in some cases may even exacerbate them. The abandonment of spirituality may be part of the problem, but more important is a lack of balance and the tendency to swing from one extreme to the other instead of finding a more sensible middle ground. Fortunately, there exist spiritual tools to help solve this problem, and one of the most potent is the system known as the Tree of Life.

The Tree of Life concept derives from an ancient system of Jewish mysticism known as Kabbalah (or Qabalah, is it is usually spelled in pagan circles). I confess that I don't know much about modern Judaism, but I gather that teaching of these concepts has largely fallen out of favor and is viewed by some as a bit of an embarrassment, but the Western esoteric tradition has wholeheartedly embraced certain aspects of the Qabalah as a useful teaching and organizational tool. It entered modern pagan practice through the Hermetic Order of the Golden Dawn, who in turn took the concepts from Medieval Jewish scholars, magicians, and alchemists, helped by a nineteenth century French occultist named Eliphas Levi. Levi was the first one to attempt to systematically relate qabalistic concepts to other traditions such as the tarot and astrology, and he was a powerful influence on the development of modern paganism.

Qabalah is an enormous and challenging area of study that encompasses everything from magical uses of the Hebrew alphabet, to occult interpretations of the Old Testament, to meditative technique, to an understanding of the creation and nature of the universe itself. It is in this latter sense that pagans and occultists tend to employ the Qabalah, and with which the Tree of Life is concerned.

The Tree of Life is a diagrammatic representation of the creation of the universe. It consists of ten spheres called Sephiroth, ten distinct emanations of divine power, progressing downward from the abstract and spiritual to the mundane physical world. The Sephiroth are arranged in three columns called The Pillar of Severity, the Pillar of Mildness, and The Pillar of Mercy, from left to right. The Sephiroth on the Pillar of Severity are generally regarded as passive, receptive, or feminine, while those on the Pillar of Mercy are active, projective, and masculine. The middle pillar synthesizes the two sides into a balanced and healthy consciousness.

One of the fundamental maxims of occultism is that individual humans represent a microcosm of the universe as a whole within their minds, bodies, and souls: "as above, so below", as it is usually phrased. Thus, the Tree not only represents aspects of the external universe, but also different aspects of human consciousness. The Tree is especially useful for correlating the contents of our chaotic and sometimes disobedient minds in order to be more stable and effective actors. A lack of balance among the Sephiroth within oneself can be responsible for individual neurosis or psychosis, and it is my view that this too can account for society-wide problems such as those we are experiencing in the twenty-first century. But before we get ahead of ourselves, let's take a look at the individual Sephiroth and what they signify.

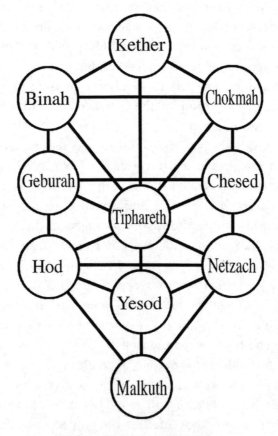

The Tree of Life

The Ten Sephiroth

Kether

Kether is the first and highest Sephira, as well as the most abstract and hardest to describe. Its name means "crown", signifying its place at the very apex of the Tree. It emerges out of nothingness and represents absolute unity, a single point within space without any other reference points by which to judge it. When people talk of god as being all things at once and one with everything, they are thinking of something like Kether. Its color is white, which contains all colors within itself. It is situated at the head of the middle pillar, representing pure divine consciousness. Unlike all the other Sephiroth, Kether has no association with heavenly bodies, but is instead related to the primordial "first swirlings" of the universe about to be created.

For practical purposes, Kether is of little use to most people, as only the most devoted and holy yogis can even hope to approach it, and none who look upon the face of god may live. Kether is often described as brilliant, limitless light, which is instructive when you realize that total light causes blindness just as sure as total darkness.

Chokmah

The second Sephira heads The Pillar of Mildness and represents the active potential of pure energy. Its color is gray and it is astrologically associated with the Zodiac (or sometimes Uranus, since that planet was discovered after the Tree of Life was formulated). In general, the right hand Pillar of Mildness corresponds to the concept of force, while the left hand Pillar of Severity relates to the idea of form, and nowhere is this contrast more evident than in the second and third Sephiroth. Following Kether's single point, Chokmah adds a second, creating spatial relations and the possibility of motion. Two points can be connected by a line, which then gives the concept of direction. Yet all of Chokmah's energy is still only potential, lacking any material or even the concept of form to coalesce around and act on.

Chokmah represents the archetypical form of chaotic, unconstrained force, which can be neither creative nor destructive until channeled into something more concrete, as we will see. The word Chokmah means "wisdom", and is symbolized by the venerable father figure.

Binah

The third Sephira heads The Pillar of Severity, and is sometimes given the title The Great Mother. It represents the archetypical idea of form, where the energy of Chokmah is limited from potential into actual. With Binah, a third point is added to the previous two, and now instead of a line we can draw a two-dimension figure, the first visual representation of form. Binah's color is black and it is associated with the planet Saturn. Saturn is rather a grim astrological force, corresponding to time, death, and the harvest. But the reference to death here need not be a sinister one. Every decision we make is in a sense the death of all other possible choices we could have made. In the same way, restricting Chokmah's infinite potential into a concrete form is the death of all those other potential possibilities, yet without this death no action would be possible. This is an important insight into the way that pagans in general think about death, more as a change than as an end, and yet all change is an end to the status quo.

The word Binah means understanding, and it represents a progression from Chokmah's wisdom to a more practical and less abstract application of that wisdom. Being wise in a vacuum is not especially meaningful; it is only through understanding that we can make that wisdom useful.

Chesed

The fourth Sephira falls on the right side of the Tree and is the first below a significant gap known as The Abyss. This signifies a transition from the archetypical world of the first three Sephiroth into the creative world, in which concepts become more concrete and practical. The word Chesed means "mercy", its color is blue, and it corresponds to the planet Jupiter. Jupiter was the king of the gods, and likewise Chesed is often represented as a kind and wise king, ruling his kingdom with a loving hand.

Here, we start to see associations with aspects of human consciousness, and Chesed corresponds to the imaginative faculties. Using Chesed, we can construct images in our mind, make plans for the future, and imagine things that are possible as well as actual. This is borne out geometrically as we connect a fourth point to the plane established by Binah, allowing the possibility of three-dimensional objects. Perhaps most importantly, Chesed represents the crystallization of Binah's abstract idea of form into something more concrete. We are not yet into the real world of physical objects; in Chesed such things can be thought about using the creative abilities of the imagination.

Geburah

Geburah means "strength", and it occupies the middle position on The Pillar of Severity, directly across from Chesed. This is important, as these two forces pull against each other to create a crucial balance. Mercy without strength is weakness; strength without mercy is tyranny. Both of these concepts are required for anything like justice to be achieved.

Geburah is the fifth Sephira and its number is five, its color is red, and its astrological correspondent is Mars. Consequently, this Sephira is often regarded as rather fearsome. Indeed, another title for Geburah is Pachad, which means "fear".

While Chesed was described as a wise and loving king, Geburah is the king at the head of his troops, going out to fight. Yet, it would be a mistake to think of Geburah in a purely negative sense. None of the Sephiroth are bad, but they can all cause problems if out of balance with the others. The severity of Geburah is a necessary component of any healthy psyche or society, and this can be seen by the fact that it corresponds to the human will. It is through strength of will that we are able to accomplish our goals and change things for the better. Here, the concepts developed in Chesed are put into action through the force of will. The architect's blueprints, however well-designed, are useless without a foreman willing to break earth and get his hands dirty, and that is one of the roles of Geburah.

Tiphareth

Tiphareth is the sixth Sephira and occupies the middle position on the Tree, both horizontally and vertically. Its color is yellow and it corresponds to both the Sun that gives us life and light and the son to Chokmah's father. In Christian mysticism, this would be the part of the Holy Trinity occupied by Christ. In Tiphareth is where we find human individuality, personality, and consciousness.

The word Tiphareth means "beauty", which is appropriate for its equilibration and mediation of the extremes on the two outer pillars. Here, the strength of Geburah and the mercy of Chesed are synthesized into justice. This is in accordance with the Aristotelian idea that virtue lies in finding the middle path between two extremes. The beauty of Tiphareth lies in its balance and combination of diverse forces to make a greater whole.

Netzach

The seventh Sephira is called Netzach, which means victory. It sits at the base of The Pillar of Mercy, and here we see the energy of Chokmah passed down through the creative crystallization of Chesed to become rampant. Remember that as we move further down the Tree, the forces become more material and less abstract. Some have used words like degraded or corrupted to describe this progression, but there's nothing inherently corrupt about matter. It's just that it's easier to abuse material forces than archetypical ones, and the damage caused by such abuse is more noticeable to those of us living in the material world.

Netzach's color is green, which is appropriate given that I often imagine its energies as plants growing wild. If we think about jungles, kudzu, and creeping vines we can easily see how the Netzach's energy can quickly get out of control. Here, imbalance can be particularly destructive, so it's important that Netzach's energies are balanced by their opposite, which we will come to next. Astrologically, Netzach corresponds to Venus, the goddess of love, and within the human psyche it corresponds to the emotions. Here again, we see that these forces are not simple to summarize. Emotions are beautiful and an important part of what it means to be human, and love is the greatest and most powerful emotion. But it's obvious that the very things that make love precious also make it dangerous, and just like a garden unpruned can take over and destroy an area, love unchecked can devour and destroy an individual.

It's worth noting here that, while The Pillar of Mercy is traditionally represented as masculine, Venus, love, and the emotions are stereotypically associated with the feminine. This just goes to show the limits of language to construct these correspondences. Masculine and feminine are imperfect descriptors of the two outer pillars, but are nevertheless useful in helping to illustrate polarity and balance. While we can argue about Venus being female and Mars being male, it's clear that the energy of strong emotions is active and projective, which are important qualities of the right-hand pillar, while the limiting severity of Geburah holding mercy in check is more passive and receptive. Masculinity and femininity are archetypes, not descriptions of objective reality. On the individual level, each of us is made up of a complex mixture of masculine and feminine influences, regardless of our biological sex, and it would be a mistake to oversimplify or stereotype based on these archetypical forces.

As far as the Tree is concerned, it's important not to get too hung up on any individual correspondence, and I know that many people are increasingly turning away from the male-female polarity model entirely. I have retained it here both for the sake of tradition and because I continue to find instructive value in it.

Hod

The eighth Sephira is called Hod and sits at the base of The Pillar of Severity. Its name means "glory", its color is orange, and it is associated with the planet Mercury. In classical mythology, Mercury was the messenger of the gods, and Hod is therefore associated with writing and communication. In the human consciousness, it corresponds to the intellect, and for this reason it also has associations with thought, study, and the magical arts themselves. Mercury's Egyptian counterpart Thoth was the god of magic, and was said to have invented writing, so it's no surprise that Thoth is also commonly mentioned in connection with Hod.

While intellectual pursuits may seem abstract initially, Hod's position on the Tree shows that mere logic and rationalism are actually quite low on the spiritual hierarchy, and much closer to the material world than we might have assumed. The higher Sephiroth representing will, creativity, and consciousness itself demonstrate that there are aspects of humanity that far exceed rational thought in terms of spiritual purity. In Hod, the form concept first developed in Binah is brought close to the realm of matter by the straight lines and clear organization necessary for logic and reason to operate.

Yesod

Yesod means "foundation" and rests, appropriately enough, near the base of the middle pillar of the Tree. Only the material world, which we will come to next, hangs below it. Yesod is the spiritual foundation on which the rest of the Tree is built, where the creative world of the previous five Sephiroth condenses down into the world of formation, and we draw ever nearer to our mundane reality. Yesod's number is nine, its color is purple, and its planetary attribution is to the moon. The moon is traditionally viewed as a mysterious, watery entity that controls the tides and affects our dreams. Accordingly, Yesod resides just beyond our normal consciousness in what psychologists would call the subconscious. It is in the realm of Yesod that psychic phenomena are said to take place, and where we can most easily make contact with non-physical entities such as ghosts, spirits, and faeries.

Like all the Sephiroth on the middle pillar, Yesod is a balancing or equilibrating force, uniting the two opposing tendencies of Hod and Netzach into something new. Both reason and emotion are essential to any firm foundation, and creating that foundation is part of the function that Yesod fulfills.

Malkuth

The tenth and final Sephira is called Malkuth, which means "kingdom". It hangs pendant from Yesod at the base of The Pillar of Mildness and represents the material world as we experience it. Most people spend the majority of their lives, apart from dreams and reveries, firmly rooted in Malkuth, blissfully unaware that the other spheres even exist, even though our psyches are certainly affected by all of them. It is in Malkuth that the grand process of creation comes to fulfillment, but don't make the mistake of thinking of it as an end. According to Qabalistic thought, divine energy continuously flows down the Tree of Life at all times, and without it the universe would cease to exist. In this sense, creation is not a single act, but an ongoing process that continues indefinitely.

To Malkuth, the planet Earth is assigned, and instead of one color it is given four: citrine, olive, russet, and black. Because its number and the total number of the Sephiroth is ten, this number is given special significance in occult circles, and is sometimes referred to as the number of completion. It represents total fulfilment of a process to its logical conclusion. Yet, at its place at the base of The Pillar of Mildness, Malkuth also represents a starting place for those who wish to elevate their consciousness to higher levels and embark on a voyage of spiritual development.

So What?

The preceding is an extremely condensed summary of a phenomenally complex topic about which hundreds of volumes have been written. The Further Reading section in the back of this book contains many excellent resources for those who wish to learn more, but for now I suppose you're wondering why I am wasting your time with all this esoteric mumbo jumbo and what any of this has to do with libertarian political philosophy. Fair enough.

The lessons to be learned from the Tree of Life are endless, but a key takeaway for me is the importance of balance and the dangers of extremes both in one's personal life and in society at large. There are those who view society itself as a kind of independent organism, and while in my view this way of thinking can lead to the kind of dangerous collectivism that characterized the major wars of the twentieth century, it is nevertheless worth considering the ways in which the consciousness of individuals can be collected together in large groups which can have an impact on society and culture. If we view the United States at the time of this writing (the summer of 2021) in qabalistic terms, I think we can draw some important conclusions about what's going on and how to solve some of our largest problems.

Put simply, it seems to me that what we are witnessing is largely a reaction to a societal imbalance towards the left side of the Tree, and a subsequent overcorrection towards the right side. We can see this most clearly in a couple of specific examples. The one which I find most obvious is the conflict between Geburah (strength) and Chesed (mercy). For a long time, the criminal justice system has been broken, characterized by overly punitive attitudes towards crime, carried out by an overly militarized police force. Little effort was put into understanding or empathizing with criminals, examining why they behave the way they do, or even questioning whether their so-called crimes should even be illegal in the first place. Instead, America embraced an arrest first, ask questions later, tough on crime mindset that disproportionately impacted those with the least power in society, and landed millions of people behind bars for victimless crimes.

For anyone who resisted this system, it was open season, as we saw case after case of police killing suspects in the streets. Few people cared, because we had been told that resisting arrest, even a wrongful arrest, was itself a crime worthy of a death sentence. This situation can be accurately described as an overdevelopment of the forces contained in Geburah: severity without mercy. But with the ubiquity of cell phone cameras, more and more people gradually became aware of what was going on, and a reaction predictably emerged. The summer of 2020 witnessed nationwide protests, many of which turned into violent riots, expressing anger at the killing of George Floyd, Breonna Taylor, Eric Garner, and other African Americans who had died in confrontations with law enforcement. These were accompanied by calls to abolish the police and the formation of lawless "autonomous zones" in major cities, which quickly devolved into poverty, squalor, and violent infighting. Somewhere along the way, the message that black lives matter got lost as predominantly black neighborhoods were trashed and black-owned businesses were looted. Protestors were responding to legitimate grievances, but instead of making things better they seemed to be making them worse. Why was this the case?

My theory is that, observing the overly strict and legalistic forces of Geburah at work, Americans fled unthinkingly to the other side of the Tree, the mercy of Chesed. Instead of justice, they embraced lawlessness and chaos. Recall that The Pillar of Mercy is characterized by the archetypical idea of force, as opposed to the form of The Pillar of Severity. The reason we saw such violence and destruction was that this force was unleashed without being tempered by at least a little of the restraint provided by Geburah. One imbalance was replaced with another, and the result was predictably messy.

Moving down the Tree, we can see another example involving the dual Sephiroth Netzach and Hod. For the last several centuries, the wake of the Enlightenment has put a high priority on logic, reason, objective truth, the scientific method, along with the suppression of superstition and emotional intelligence. Things that were not provable under laboratory conditions were considered unimportant or even dangerous, and traditional institutions fell under attack as well-educated elites believed they could use their new tools to devise a better way.

I do not mean this as an attack on the Enlightenment or its values; quite the contrary. Advances in medicine, labor-saving technology, and an unprecedented alleviation of poverty have largely sprung from the embrace of science and reason in the Western world. As a person who is pretty analytically-minded myself, if I err it is definitely on the side of Hod. Yet, it seems that there is a cost to shunning emotion and intuition too severely. An overreliance on Hod creates a vacuum in Netzach, which must then be filled by an overcorrection in the opposite direction (see how neatly Newton's laws of motion are followed even in the metaphysical realm?) The reaction can be seen in a trend emerging from academia almost towards nihilism. Building on (and some might say distorting) the ideas of postmodern philosophy, this new way of thinking (slangily called "wokeness" by those who oppose it) has attempted to break down all the walls erected by reason. Because perfectly certain knowledge is not possible, the cult of wokeness denies the existence of truth itself. Objective reality is replaced by a total relativism in which there are no such things as good and evil, right and wrong. A side effect, and indeed a necessary condition for it, is that internal contradictions must be tolerated. This is justified by the claim that the laws of logic themselves are nothing more than tools of oppressors, in which case reasoning is impossible and there's no point in even trying.

This is why you can find people simultaneously defending cultures that regularly execute homosexuals while at the same time condemning as irredeemable bigots perfectly peaceful Americans with exclusively heterosexual dating preferences. It's why you see people railing against the patriarchy's oppression and exclusion of women one minute, and demanding policies that will lead to the abolition of female sports leagues in the next. It doesn't matter if it doesn't make sense; it only matters whether it feels right. The rampant emotions of Netzach are beginning to take over from the cold rationalism of Hod, and the overcorrection merely reverses the imbalance without fixing it.

Although there are obvious exceptions, broadly speaking the political Left seems more aligned with The Pillar of Mercy and the political Right seem more committed to The Pillar of Severity, at least in the present moment. This can help explain why political polarization is so noticeably stark right now. The two sides are not merely fighting over a set of policies, but over an entire approach to how they view and interact with the world.

Libertarianism and Balance

Libertarians understand that neither the approach of the Right nor of the Left is the correct one. Both make the same error, albeit in the opposite direction. The solution to too much head is not too much heart, the solution to an excess of strictness is not an excess of licentiousness. Instead, the two poles must be balanced against each other in harmony. The rock band Rush, whose lyrics were influenced by libertarian ideas, addressed this in their 20-minute progressive epic *Hemispheres*, which tells of society at continual war between the impassive Apollonian rationalists and the wild Dionysian hedonists. The conflict can only be resolved by arrival of Cygnus, the god of balance, to unite the hearts and minds of the citizens. Who ever said rock music just had to be about sex and drugs?

Do not suppose, however, that this attitude makes libertarians a bunch of milquetoast moderates, looking for the middle ground on every policy issue simply in order to make peace. Libertarians, as I'm sure you've gathered by now, can be very passionate and opinionated about a whole range of political issues. To return to the first example, libertarians have been strenuously arguing for major criminal justice reforms for years. We recognize that the present system is overly punitive, discriminatory, and fails to address the root causes of crime. But instead of calling for abolishing the police and allowing all criminals to go free, we propose a series of reforms that blend compassion with the strength to stand up to wrongdoing, what some might call simply "justice." By taking victimless crimes off the books, demilitarizing the police, and replacing some prison sentences with a system that requires criminals to make some sort of amends to their victims while still participating in society, we believe that crime can be reduced while also minimizing casualties and injustice at the hands of police and courts. Similarly, we believe in having compassion for marginalized groups and supporting their rights, without imposing an authoritarian regime of compliance on everyone else, or defending brutal tyranny around the globe. These are just two examples, but if you run through the list of controversial policies, you will generally find that libertarians denounce both conservative and progressive solutions in favor of ones that strike a balance between mercy and severity, between heart and mind.

The study of Qabalah and the Tree of Life is not an essential feature of many forms of paganism, but it does have a long tradition of use both in Wicca and in the ceremonial magic from which it partially derives. Personally, I find it to be the most instructive esoteric tool I have encountered for making sense of the world and for guiding me on my own spiritual journey, but everyone's path is different, and if the Qabalah holds no appeal to you, there's no need to incorporate it into either your practice or your worldview.

Embracing the Shadow

Continuing the theme of polarity and balance, we should take a few minutes to talk about shadow work. Some may be familiar with this idea from Jungian psychology. Carl Jung was something of a mystic and very interested in subjects such as alchemy and astrology, so it's no surprise that his explorations of the human mind shares much in common with pagan and occult understandings of consciousness. One of the key insights of all these traditions is that each of us has a dark side, or shadow self, which we typically work hard to bury and suppress deep within ourselves. This is quite understandable. The shadow self can be a pretty nasty character whose emergence can result in undesirable consequences ranging from embarrassment to complete destruction. As in Robert Louis Stevenson's classic novel Dr. Jekyll and Mr. Hyde, the polite, productive, and restrained face we present to the world is counterbalanced by a wild and animalistic aspect that most of us would find appalling to behold.

This basic truth is complicated by a paradox: those who fail to confront their shadows become their shadows. In other words, if you don't face up to and deal with all the things you hate about yourself, they will end up manifesting outwardly in some very unpleasant ways. The term "shadow work" refers to this confrontation and reconciliation between the light and dark aspects of the personality. The wise recognize that you can never destroy your shadow. Neither can you keep it buried forever. You must accept it and find ways to incorporate it productively into your life. The failure to do so can lead to neurosis, unhappiness, and hypocrisy. Shadow work forms an important part of pagan spiritual development.

The existence of certain stereotypes about pagans means that it's important to be clear about what this means. You may have noticed that many pagans seem to be attracted to a dark aesthetic that can be frightening to people unfamiliar with it. Gathering in black cloaks in dark forests, surrounded by bats and ravens, to pay respect to the moon, and other such gothic trappings, are certainly part of the appeal. This is partially because these things are simply really cool and we like them. On the other hand, the darkness of many pagan traditions has to do with our more open relationship with the shadow side of human psychology, a side that tends to be suppressed in other religions.

Shadow work is not a license to be wicked, nor does it involve sacrificing animals, orgiastic rituals, or any of the horror movie tropes you may have seen surrounding pagans. Although I thoroughly enjoy films like *The Wicker Man* or *Midsommer*, Hollywood has been no friend to the reputation of paganism over the years. As discussed in Chapter 2, pagans are bound by ethics just the same as anyone else, and the ideas spread by Satanic Panic propaganda are simply myths. Shadow work simply acknowledges the indisputable fact that we are not angels, and attempts to accommodate and adapt to that fact rather than deny it. Moreover, a thorough understanding of your own dark side will help prevent outbursts of violence and neuroticism that we sometimes see among those with poor self-awareness. As the ancient Greek proverb wisely insists: *know thyself.*

Libertarians are also well aware of humanity's dark side. In fact, one of the most frequent criticisms of communist or socialist economic systems from a libertarian perspective is that they fail to account for the incentives that motivate human behavior. Like it or not, self-interest is a primary driver of how we behave, and any system that depends on people acting against their own self-interest is not likely to be very successful. Communism expects its workers to toil without financial reward, for the good of the party or the nation. Those who shirk receive the same wages as those who exert maximum effort. It doesn't take a genius to see that self-interest points to more shirking and less working, and the history of communist regimes bears this out. Likewise, we expect political leaders to be selfless and public-spirited, when in fact they invariably turn their power towards enriching themselves and destroying their enemies. We can lament this state of affairs, but lamenting it does not change it.

In contrast to the wishful thinking of utopians, the Scottish economist Adam Smith observed that, in a market economy, we benefit from the work of others not because of their good intentions or their charity, but because of their self-interest. It is not from the benevolence of the butcher, he said, that we expect our daily meal. Instead, he provides us with food for our tables because he is able to profit from doing so. In this way, the market system accommodates the fact of self-interest, while bending it towards the benefit of others. These sorts of observations have led to many people accusing libertarianism of being a selfish ideology, celebrating a cutthroat competitive environment where dog eats dog and it's every man for himself. This is a case of shooting the messenger. Markets do not create selfishness; selfishness exists in all economic systems, and is an inherent fact of what it means to be human. What markets do is give that already extant selfishness a productive outlet through which it can be made to help others. One remarkable feature of a free market that no one ever talks about is that it's actually impossible to make money without doing good for someone else. If you want to get rich, you have to offer a product or a service that people badly need or want. By fulfilling those needs and wants, you are making society a better place at the same time as you enrich yourself. Contrast this with a system in which wealth can be obtained through political favors, extortion, threats, legislation, confiscation, fines, bribes, and kickbacks – a system like that of the former Soviet Union – and tell me which appears the more virtuous. To the libertarian, the answer is obvious.

This recognition and accommodation of the darker aspects of human nature is the political equivalent to the spiritual shadow work a pagan has to do if he wishes to overcome his demons. If we don't want society to become consumed by its own shadow, we have to work to reconcile with it. When we see people preaching tolerance while practicing hate, extolling peace while practicing war, demanding freedom while trying to oppress and dominate others, you can be sure that the offending parties have not come to terms with their own shadows, and are in the process of becoming the opposite of the person they claim to be.

Conclusion

Do What Thou Wilt Shall Be
the Whole of the Law

The thesis of this book is that libertarians and pagans are natural allies. It's a conclusion I've reached after listening to many conversations over the years in which I hear the same ideas expressed, albeit in different language, from both camps. Just the other day I was marveling to listen to a group of pagans talking about personal responsibility in terms that could have easily fit into any libertarian circle I've ever been a part of. "If only they knew!" I thought. It's my hope that with the publication of this book, they will know, or at least some of them will.

One of the things I love about both communities is their resistance towards being hemmed in by labels, boundaries, organizations, gatekeeping, and prescribed behavior. Getting libertarians or pagans organized is a lot like herding cats, and since I absolutely adore cats for all their ridiculous intractability, I only mean that as a compliment. As we saw in Chapter 1, both pagans and libertarians delight in being a diverse bunch with almost as many sub-categories as there are individual members. Attempts at unity invariably fail, because no one wants to be told what or how to think. It's easy to view this as a downside, and part of the reason both groups remain in the extreme minority, but personally I find such recalcitrant attitudes quite charming, speaking to a preference for principle over expediency and an inherent stubbornness that I recognize within myself as well.

There are several amusing stories illustrating the recalcitrant characteristic of libertarian paganism. In 1974, the pagan publisher Llewellyn made a naïve and foolhardy attempt to assemble the Council of American Witches, with the goal of formalizing some definitions of what the religion consisted of and to agree on some common principles. But after some encouraging initial progress, the Council of American Witches quickly fell apart over irreconcilable internal differences. A letter from one obstinately anonymous witch sums up, at least for me, the attitude of the broader community:

> *In the early days of the Church, we of the Wicca were persecuted for not joining with the common belief of the church father because we refused to join, be baptized or pay our tithes to their God. We were tortured, burned, hanged and placed in vats of ground glass. We preferred to live simply, worshipping our old Gods of Harvest, and doing as we had for years before, and as our fathers had done....*
>
> *The Church sent in spies who reported on us into our worship circles, and those of us who were caught were humiliated and killed because we were who we were....and of course the Church wanted the money and wanted to oppress the people.*
>
> *Now it seems to us old Wicca that that is what you younger's are doing... oppressing us, trying to force us to join in an organization, and criticizing us for wanting our freedom and our belief in freedom....*
>
> *Let us not quarrel among ourselves. Leave us be and we shall do the same for you. worship as you see best and allow us also the same right. This is the true Wicca way....and the free way.*[12]

This commitment to the ideas of live and let live, minding your own business, and not trying to impose definitions or rules onto a community that had been getting along perfectly well without them is wholly in keeping with libertarian principles, and many a libertarian organization has suffered the same fate as the Council of American Witches, and for the same reasons. Still, the fact that the popular media continues to nurture a certain amount of hostility towards both groups despite their almost total lack of numbers, political power, or cultural influence would seem to point to something profound behind our ideas, profound enough to be threatening to the status quo. Maybe it's just my contrarian nature, but I find that comforting.

Pagans and libertarians may be strange bedfellows, but they are bedfellows indeed, both poorly understood and attacked by those who find their ideas in some way dangerous. But it's also still the case that many pagans hold a stereotyped view of the libertarian as standing against everything they believe in: a selfish, materialistic, agent of environmental destruction with no empathy for the suffering of others. Likewise, there are plenty of libertarians who still think of pagans as goat-slaughtering, Satan-worshipping flakes obsessed with ridiculous superstitions. I'm hoping to have dispelled a few of those myths here, partly by directly confronting them, but mainly by demonstrating the shared set of ethics and value that underlie these two beautiful and sympathetic worldviews.

We're living in a time when people are increasingly divided, unwilling to listen and eager to wall off anyone who dares to express a differing opinion. In such an environment I think we could all benefit from a little more openness and understanding. If this book helps two groups of people of whom I am very fond understand one another just a little bit better, I will consider that a success. As I said at the outset, I'm not interested in telling anyone how to vote or which religion to practice. You have to find those answers for yourself. But the fact that we want everyone to have the freedom to search for those answers is what unites us. I don't know about you, but I'd like to see a world with a little bit more unity and less division. Mutual understanding is the first step in creating that world.

Blessed be,

– Logan Albright

January 2022, Washington, DC

About the Author

Logan Albright is a writer, musician, filmmaker, libertarian, and occultist who has spent the last decade in Washington, DC. He serves as the Head Writer for Free the People Foundation, which seeks to use visual storytelling to communicate libertarian ideas, and is an initiate of the DC-area pan-pagan organization The Firefly House.

Logan's previous books include *Conform or Be Cast Out: The (Literal) Demonization of Nonconformists* and *Our Servants, Our Masters: How Control Masquerades as Assistance*. In the former of these, he defends the nonconforming individual from the disturbingly frequent charge that to be different is to somehow be demonic, while in the latter he deconstructs the idea of the "public servant", a slippery character who more often than not would rather rule humanity than serve it.

If you enjoyed this book and are interested in more of Logan's work, please visit www.loganalbright.com. Direct questions, comments, or complaints can be addressed to logan.albright@gmail.com.

Notes

1. Benjamin Fearnow, "Number of Witches Rises Dramatically Across the U.S.as Millennials Reject Christianity", *Newsweek,* November 18, 2018. https://www.newsweek.com/witchcraft-wiccans-mysticism-astrology-witches-millennials-pagans-religion-1221019 (accessed January 19, 2022)

2. Penny Billington, *The Path of Druidry,* p. 285, Llewellyn Publications, 2016.

3. Robin Wood, *When, Why ...If,* p. 89, Livingtree Books, 2018.

4. Gemma Gary, *The Devil's Dozen: Thirteen Craft Rites of the Old One,* pp 10-11, Troy Books Publishing, 2015.

5. John Milton, *Paradise Lost,* Lines 255-257.

6. Mircea Eliade, *A History of Religious Ideas, Volume 1,* p. 181, The University of Chicago Press, 1981.

7. Matthew 22:21

8. Margot Adler, *Drawing Down the Moon,* p. 401, Penguin Books, 2006.

9. Robin Wood, *When, Why ...If,* p. 100, Livingtree Books, 2018.

10. Robin Wood, *When, Why ...If,* p. 49, Livingtree Books, 2018.

11. Heather Greene, "Paganism, gods and goddesses aside, is the most LGBTQ-affirming faith in the US", *The Washington Post,* July 12, 2021.

12. Quoted in Margot Adler, *Drawing Down the Moon,* p. 96, Penguin Books, 2006.

Further Reading

Whether you are a libertarian interested in paganism or a pagan interested in libertarianism, it is my hope that this book will leave you wanting more information on either or both topics. Of course, both subjects are vast in scope, with long and involved histories, but here are a few resources to get you started. You'll soon find that once you start walking down the path, it extends for as far as you care to go (and even farther).

Further Reading on Libertarianism

For a general introduction to libertarian thought, I recommend *The Libertarian Mind* by David Boaz, which is an efficient entry-level text that guides the reader through the logic of libertarian ideas, and applies them to the problems we face in the world. In this same vein, I strongly recommend *Don't Hurt People and Don't Take Their Stuff* by Matt Kibbe, a libertarian manifesto for the layperson that lays out the ideas of personal freedom in an easy and approachable style.

Speaking of manifestoes, I can't go without mentioning Murray Rothbard's *For a New Liberty*, an Earth-shaking work that takes libertarian ideas to their logical conclusion. If you are inclined towards the more radical side of political philosophy, you will surely find much of interest in this book. Slightly less iconoclastic, but equally essential is Friedrich Hayek's *The Constitution of Liberty*. Hayek was an Austrian economist and recipient of the Nobel Prize. His work was instrumental in the intellectual resistance to the totalitarian regimes that were gaining power in Europe during his lifetime. *The Constitution of Liberty* is the culmination of his political and economic philosophy into one, admittedly hefty, volume. Also of note is Hayek's *The Fatal Conceit*, which seeks to explain why and how political leaders always overestimate their own knowledge and ability to solve complex problems from the top down.

For an introduction to the libertarian view on economics, you can hardly do better than *Economics in One Lesson* by Henry Hazlitt, which explains the fundamental principle of why a laissez-faire approach generally yields superior results. This book is a reworking of an older essay by French economist Frederic Bastiat called *That Which Is Seen and That Which Is Not Seen*, which is also a very good read. If you want to go deeper in this direction, the two works I would recommend are *Human Action* and *Epistemological Problems in Economics* both by Ludwig von Mises. *Human Action* is probably the closest thing libertarian economics has to a Bible, and it reads like one, being incredibly long and detailed, but if you can get through it, it's a masterpiece. *Epistemological Problems* deals with the mistake of applying the methods of the physical sciences to the social sciences, a mistake which underlies the scientism that led to so many human tragedies throughout the twentieth century. I promise it's less boring than it sounds.

Finally, for a somewhat outdated, but still highly worthwhile attempt to derive a set of libertarian ethics from the ground up, I am quite fond of *Principles of Ethics* by Herbert Spencer. Spencer was an English philosopher who sought to understand the world through the then newly emerging lens of evolutionary biology, and it is from that perspective that he addresses the questions of ethics. Being fundamentally materialistic in his approach, he is not entirely successful, but I still regard him as a towering thinker whose contributions to the libertarian philosophy cannot be overlooked.

Further Reading on Paganism

For a very general overview of pagan practice and belief, I recommend *Paganism: An Introduction to Earth Centered Religions* by Joyce and River Higginbotham. From there you will probably want to select a particular direction to explore further, since the topic is so broad. For example, if you find yourself attracted to the druids and their Celtic, nature-based approach to paganism, *The Path of Druidry* by Penny Billington is an excellent starting point.

If, on the other hand, you're more drawn to Wicca and witchcraft, there is an embarrassment of riches in terms of helpful resources, and it can be difficult to know where to begin. You may be tempted to start with Wicca's foundational text *Witchcraft for Today* by Gerald Gardner. I would advise against this however, as Gardner was writing at a time when even talking about witchcraft in England was barely legal, and his audience was still highly fearful and ignorant of paganism in general. This book is therefore less helpful than it might have been had it been written in a more open and receptive time. As a case in point, *Witchcraft for Tomorrow,* written some years later by Gardner's former colleague, Doreen Valiente, is an excellent introduction to Wicca that still feels relevant and informative today. I'd also recommend *Wicca: A Guide for the Solitary Practitioner* by Scott Cunningham. The title is a reference to the fact that, at the time, Wicca was generally practiced in groups, with elaborate initiation ceremonies required before newcomers could be taught the ways of the craft. This kind of secrecy was a holdover from the days when practicing witchcraft was illegal, but it persisted for decades as part of the mystique of this "forbidden religion". Cunningham did the world a service by demystifying Wicca and allowing those without a convenient pagan network to put its ideas into their personal spiritual practice.

For a history of how pagan ideas came to be revived and practiced in the twentieth century, as well as a broad survey of contemporary pagan attitudes towards a wide variety of issues, Margot Adler's *Drawing Down the Moon* remains a foundational text documenting the movement and its growth, particularly in North America.

For a look into the word of traditional British witchcraft, as distinct from Wicca, I recommend *Traditional Witchcraft: A Cornish Book of Ways* by Gemma Gary, which outlines the beliefs and practices which can still be found in parts of the author's native Cornwall, and which have persisted there from time immemorial.

If you're interested in exploring the ritual magic side of paganism, *Modern Magick* by Donald Michael Kraig is a good place to start. It's laid out as a comprehensive course with lessons that will introduce the student to the basics of meditation, the Qabalah, various gods and goddesses, and, of course, the principles of magic. It may be useful to note here that the spelling "magick" is sometimes employed in occult circles to differentiate the spiritual practice from stage illusions and prestidigitation. If a book has "magick" in the title, you can be pretty sure that it won't be about card tricks and sleight of hand. In my own writing, I choose to use the traditional spelling, however, as I think we are sophisticated enough to understand that the same word can have two unrelated meanings without causing confusion. Another excellent work similar in scope to Kraig's, but closer to the original sources, is *The Tree of Life* by Israel Regardie. Regardie was the private secretary of Aleister Crowley, and while the latter's works (though brilliant) tend to be somewhat impenetrable, Regardie's books are written for a general audience.

Despite reading dozens of books on the subject, I have never encountered what I would call a good "beginner" book on the Qabalah. All the good ones are confusingly advanced and all the ones that attempt to simplify the subject are not very good. But if you read either of the previous two books, you should have enough background to understand *Mystical Qabalah* by Dion Fortune. This book straddles a nice middle ground, being comparatively lucid and extremely insightful. It remains my favorite work on the Tree of Life.

For those intrigued by the brief mention of chaos magic in Chapter 6 (and who wouldn't be?) I recommend starting with *Liber Null & Psychonaut* by Peter J. Carroll. This compilation of two books is a good introduction to chaos magic, a modern variety of occultism that dispenses with most of the traditions and trappings of the Western Mystery Tradition in favor of a more pragmatic approach. The briefly discussed "Freedom from habit" ideas are dealt with more fully here.

Finally, I would be remiss not to mention Robin Wood's *When, Why ...If*, from which I've quoted several passages. It's intended as an ethics workbook for pagans, contains many useful exercises and thought experiments, and illustrated quite nicely why I think the ethics of paganism and libertarianism fit so neatly inside one another.

MOON BOOKS

PAGANISM & SHAMANISM

What is Paganism? A religion, a spirituality, an alternative belief system, nature worship? You can fi nd support for all these defi nitions (and many more) in dictionaries, encyclopaedias, and text books of religion, but subscribe to any one and the truth will evade you. Above all Paganism is a creative pursuit, an encounter with reality, an exploration of meaning and an expression of the soul. Druids, Heathens, Wiccans and others, all contribute their insights and literary riches to the Pagan tradition. Moon Books invites you to begin or to deepen your own encounter, right here, right now.

If you have enjoyed this book, why not tell other readers by posting a review on your preferred book site.

Bestsellers from Moon Books

Keeping Her Keys
An Introduction to Hekate's Modern Witchcraft
Cyndi Brannen
*Blending Hekate, witchcraft and personal development together
to create a powerful new magickal perspective.*
Paperback: 978-1-78904-075-3 ebook 978-1-78904-076-0

Journey to the Dark Goddess
How to Return to Your Soul
Jane Meredith
*Discover the powerful secrets of the Dark Goddess and
transform your depression, grief and pain into healing
and integration.*
Paperback: 978-1-84694-677-6 ebook: 978-1-78099-223-5

Shamanic Reiki
Expanded Ways of Working with Universal Life Force Energy
Llyn Roberts, Robert Levy
*Shamanism and Reiki are each powerful ways of healing; together,
their power multiplies. Shamanic Reiki introduces techniques to
help healers and Reiki practitioners tap ancient healing wisdom.*
Paperback: 978-1-84694-037-8 ebook: 978-1-84694-650-9

Southern Cunning
Folkloric Witchcraft in the American South
Aaron Oberon
*Modern witchcraft with a Southern flair, this book is a
journey through the folklore of the American South and
a look at the power these stories hold for modern witches.*
Paperback: 978-1-78904-196-5 ebook: 978-1-78904-197-2

Bestsellers from Moon Books
Pagan Portals Series

The Morrigan
Meeting the Great Queens
Morgan Daimler
Ancient and enigmatic, the Morrigan reaches out to us.
On shadowed wings and in raven's call, meet the ancient Irish
goddess of war, battle, prophecy, death, sovereignty, and magic.
Paperback: 978-1-78279-833-0 ebook: 978-1-78279-834-7

The Awen Alone
Walking the Path of the Solitary Druid
Joanna van der Hoeven
An introductory guide for the solitary Druid, The Awen Alone will
accompany you as you explore, and seek out your own place
within the natural world.
Paperback: 978-1-78279-547-6 ebook: 978-1-78279-546-9

Moon Magic
Rachel Patterson
An introduction to working with the phases of the Moon,
what they are and how to live in harmony with the lunar
year and to utilise all the magical powers it provides.
Paperback: 978-1-78279-281-9 ebook: 978-1-78279-282-6

Hekate
A Devotional
Vivienne Moss
Hekate, Queen of Witches and the Shadow-Lands,
haunts the pages of this devotional bringing magic
and enchantment into your lives.
Paperback: 978-1-78535-161-7 ebook: 978-1-78535-162-4

Bestsellers from Moon Books
Shaman Pathways Series

The Druid Shaman
Exploring the Celtic Otherworld
Danu Forest
*A practical guide to Celtic shamanism with exercises
and techniques as well as traditional lore for
exploring the Celtic Otherworld.*
Paperback: 978-1-78099-615-8 ebook: 978-1-78099-616-5

The Celtic Chakras
Elen Sentier
*Tread the British native shaman's path,
explore the goddess hidden in the ancient stories;
walk the Celtic chakra spiral labyrinth.*
Paperback: 978-1-78099-506-9 ebook: 978-1-78099-507-6

Elen of the Ways
British Shamanism - Following the Deer Trods
Elen Sentier
*British shamanism has largely been forgotten: the reindeer
goddess of the ancient Boreal forest is shrouded in mystery...
follow her deer-trods to rediscover her old ways.*
Paperback: 978-1-78099-559-5 ebook: 978-1-78099-560-1

Deathwalking
Helping Them Cross the Bridge
Laura Perry
*An anthology focusing on deathwalking and psychopomp work:
the shamanic practice of helping the deceased's soul pass on to
the next realm.*
Paperback: 978-1-78535-818-0 ebook: 978-1-78535-819-7

Readers of ebooks can buy or view any of these bestsellers by clicking on the live link in the title. Most titles are published in paperback and as an ebook. Paperbacks are available in traditional bookshops. Both print and ebook formats are available online.

Find more titles and sign up to our readers' newsletter
http://www.johnhuntpublishing.com/paganism

Follow us on Facebook
https://www.facebook.com/MoonBooks

Follow us on Instagram
https://www.instagram.com/moonbooksjhp/

Follow us on Twitter
https://twitter.com/MoonBooksJHP

Follow us on TikTok
https://www.tiktok.com/@moonbooksjhp